(H)is-land

Roberto RUARO

Edizioni HOGWORDS

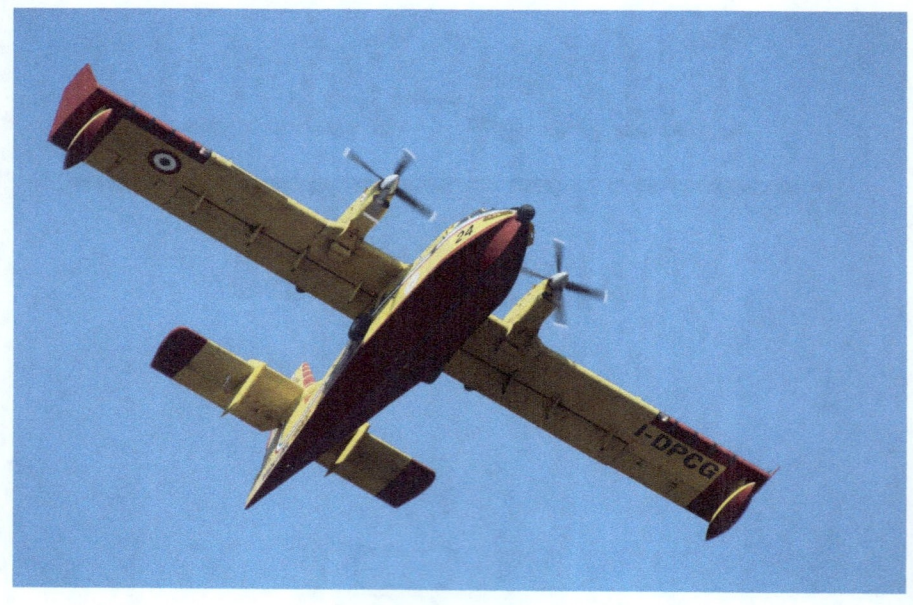

Foreword

How do you describe a shot or a photograph in simple words? I don't think it's that simple. It all depends on the viewer and the observer. Everyone sees different things in the same image. Take a cloud, for example. If you look at the sky, you can create authentic stories. Everything always starts from there, from a story. A story that tells many stories, unique and intertwined. A book, a poem, a picture, together they tell a story. Stories have an almost magical power, they have the gift of conveying feelings and emotions.

In this case, the photo book that the reader holds in his hands has the intention of sharing with all of us what its author, Roberto Ruaro, as well as a great photographer, has felt while capturing these moments. He wants to share with us his spectacular work among the shades and colours of nature and beyond.

Looking at each photo, we can admire the details and feel almost close to the moment of the shot. I can neither know nor understand what anyone might feel, but these pictures have the ability to transport us into the image.

So now I leave it to the readers to enjoy these images and wish them to let their imaginations run wild between the pages in search of the true essence of each one.

I am grateful for all the feelings that the author communicates in these pages, especially to those who will be lucky enough to see them with the eyes of the heart. I will not detain the readers any longer and wish them good reading and good viewing.

Veronica PEPOLI

Introduction

My name is Roberto Ruaro, I was born on 24 April 1968 in Albenga, where I still live. I am married with three children and a cat. I work as a surveyor and my hobby is photography. I have always been attracted by photographs, both when I see them and when I take them. I have always admired those who know how to capture the moment with a single shot, and I have quietly tried to learn and replicate it. My children have always been exposed to this passion of mine, so much so that for years I hammered them photographically...

Then I started photographing the island of Gallinara and it became my favourite subject, painted at every moment of the day, so much so that it earned me the nickname of the island photographer. In fact, at every moment of the day it gives us something different and I never get tired of it. But it's not all I do: I love sunrises, sunsets and reflections, which I see as messages from above, from our loved ones who are up there. Then I like to take a photograph when I see something special, to capture a moment forever and share it. For me, sharing is fundamental and social media can be a very useful tool. I share something from my country and someone else shares something from their country. That is really great. It was with this passion that I realised my dream of seeing a 3 x 4 metre photo of myself, depicting the island of Gallinara, exhibited at the Coop in Albenga. Since then I have created an exhibition with some of my photographs and it has been a great satisfaction.

Now the time has come to see the most beautiful dream come true: a book with my photos. It doesn't seem real to me. It is really the closing of a circle, the beginning of a period of great satisfaction, the genesis of something new, but at the moment I want to keep my feet on the ground and enjoy its realisation, hoping that it will be appreciated. I have chosen some of the photos that I think are the most beautiful, that have moved me the most. I hope to convey all that they have given me.

Love for photography
in 50 snapshots!

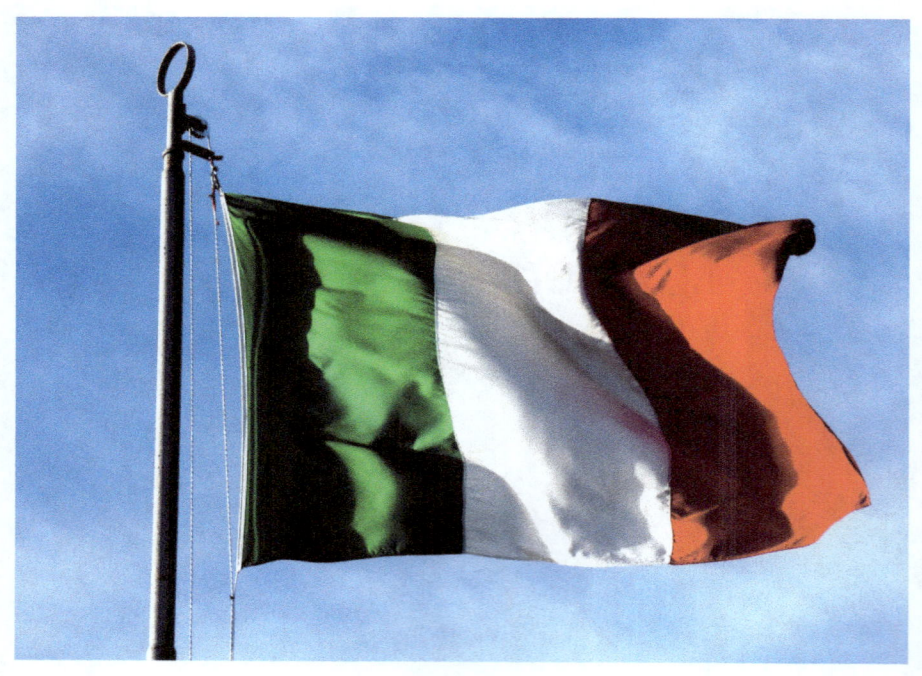

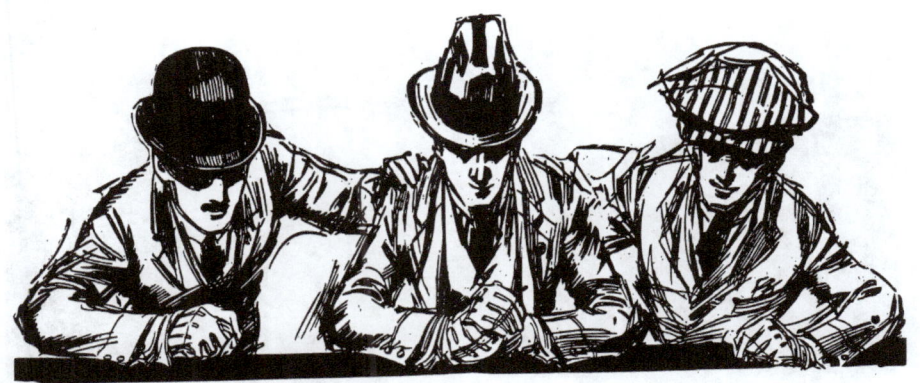

The shadows will slip behind you
if you turn your face to the sun.

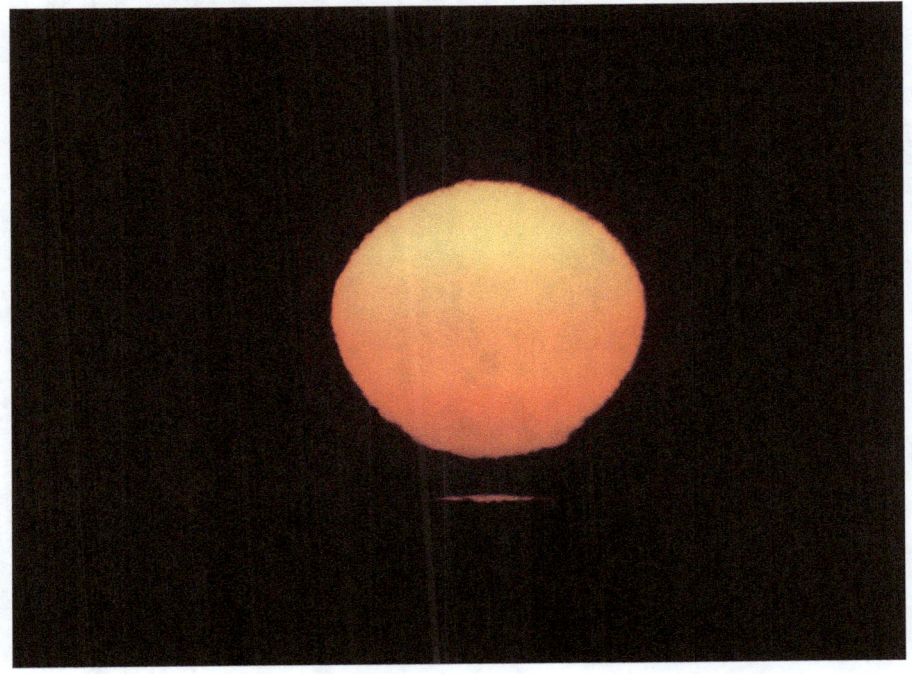

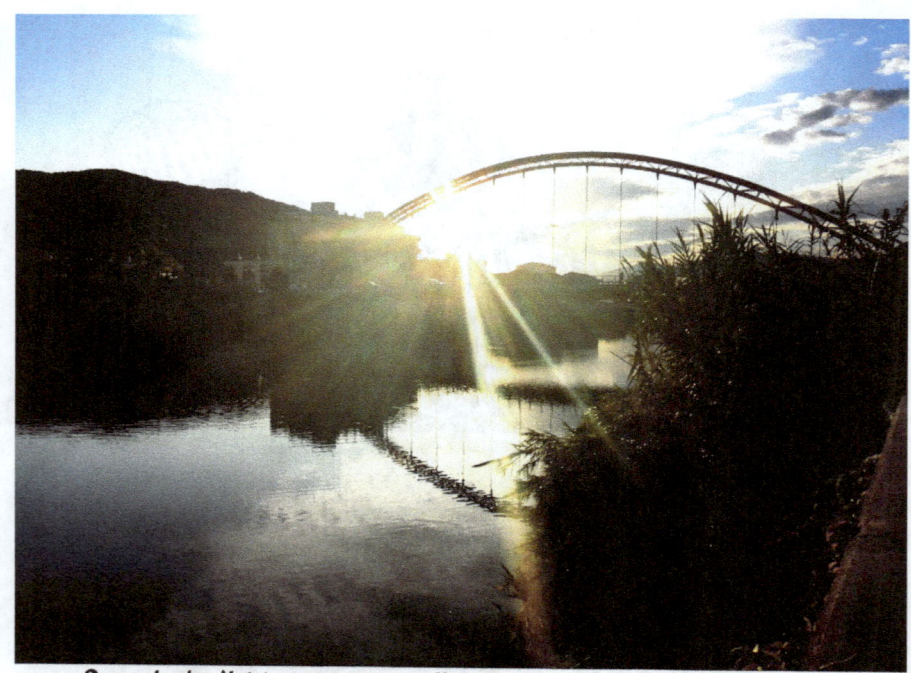

People build too many walls and never enough bridges.

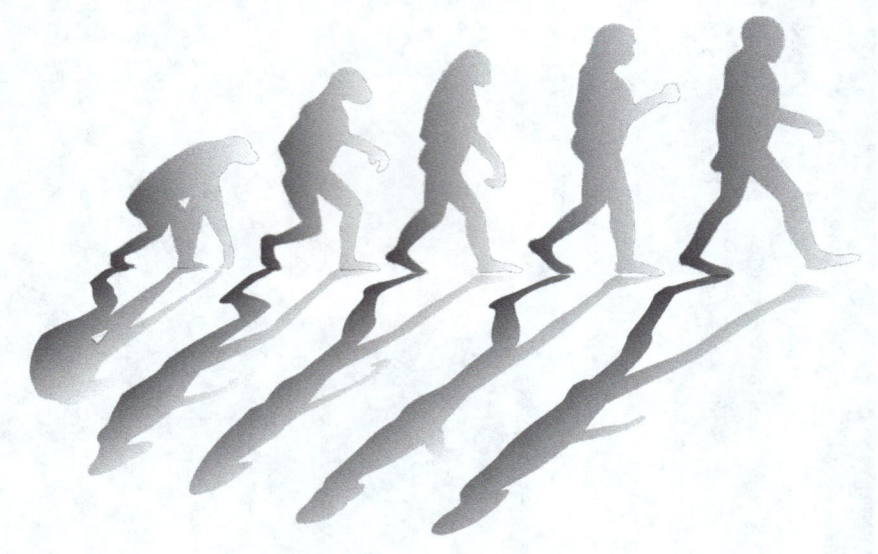

11

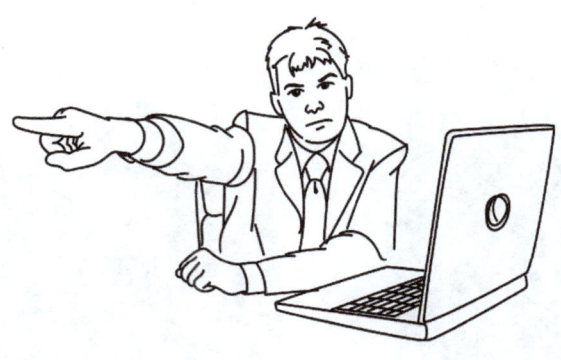

You can tell the heart of a man by the way he treats animals.

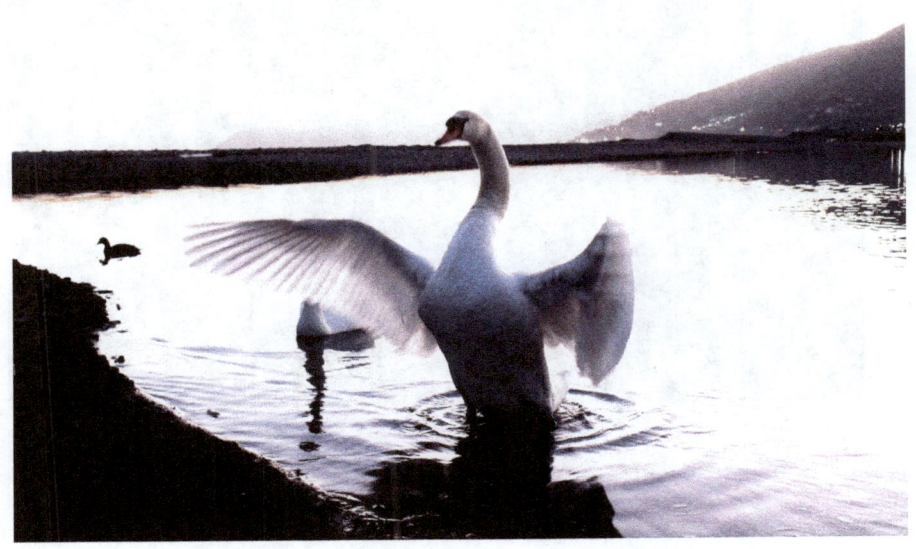

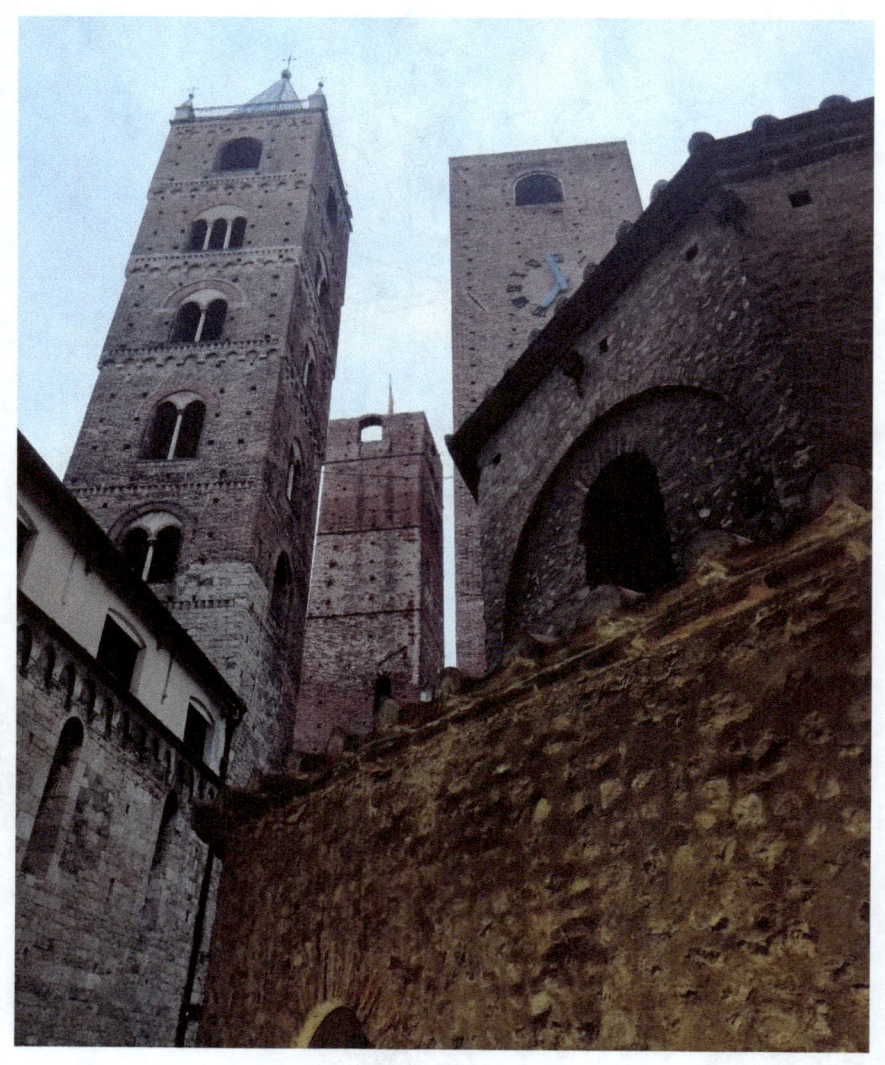

Both bells ring for the good judge.

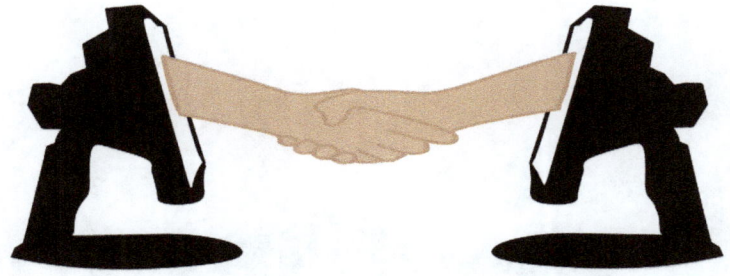

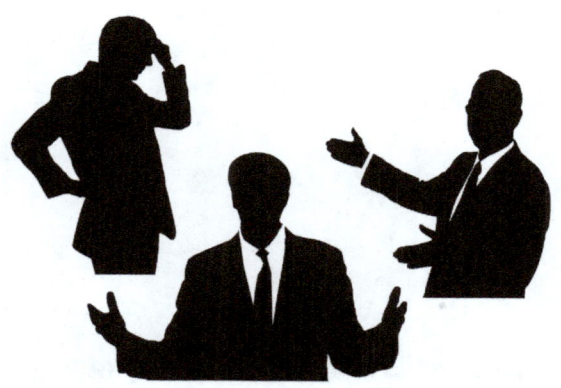

Amidst every difficulty there is an island of opportunity.

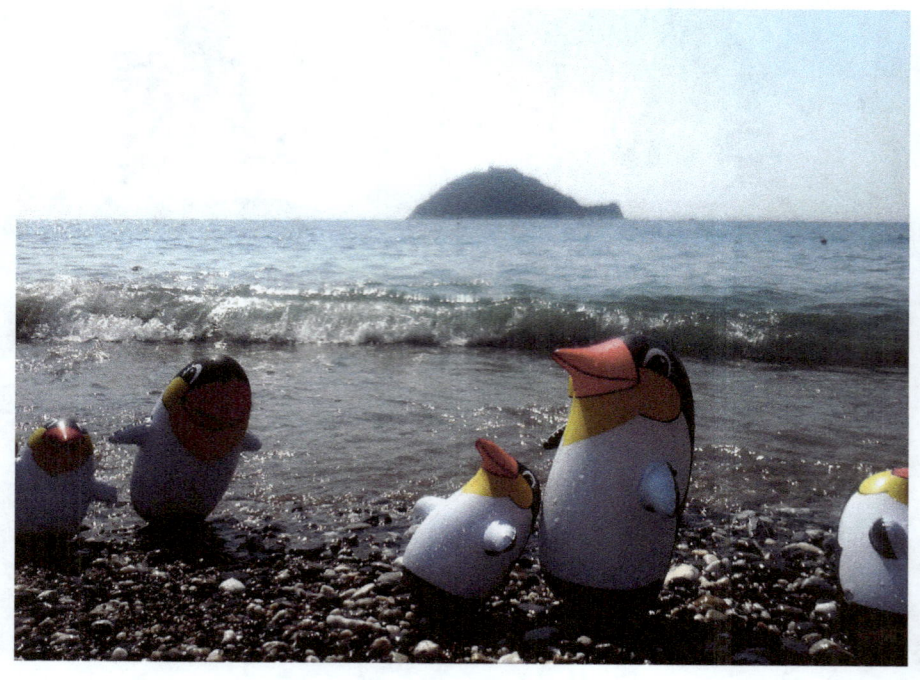

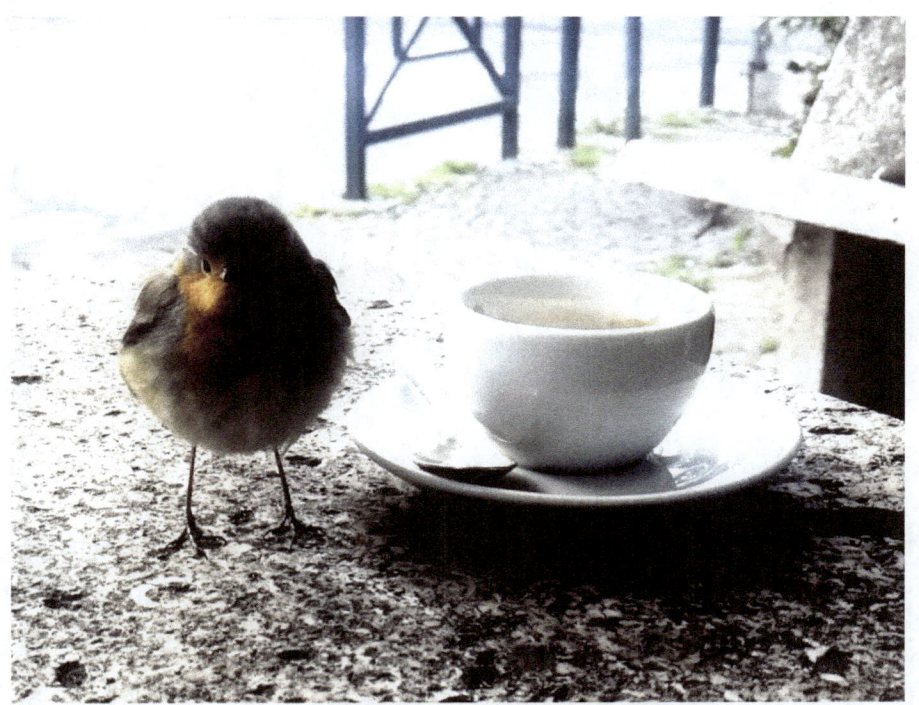

I measured my life in teaspoons of coffee.

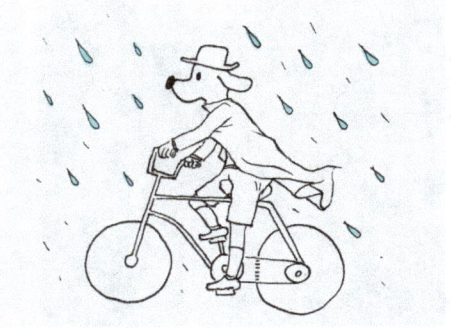

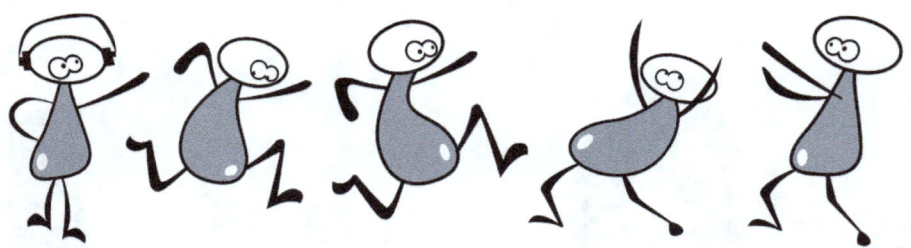

To rouse a tiger, use a long stick.

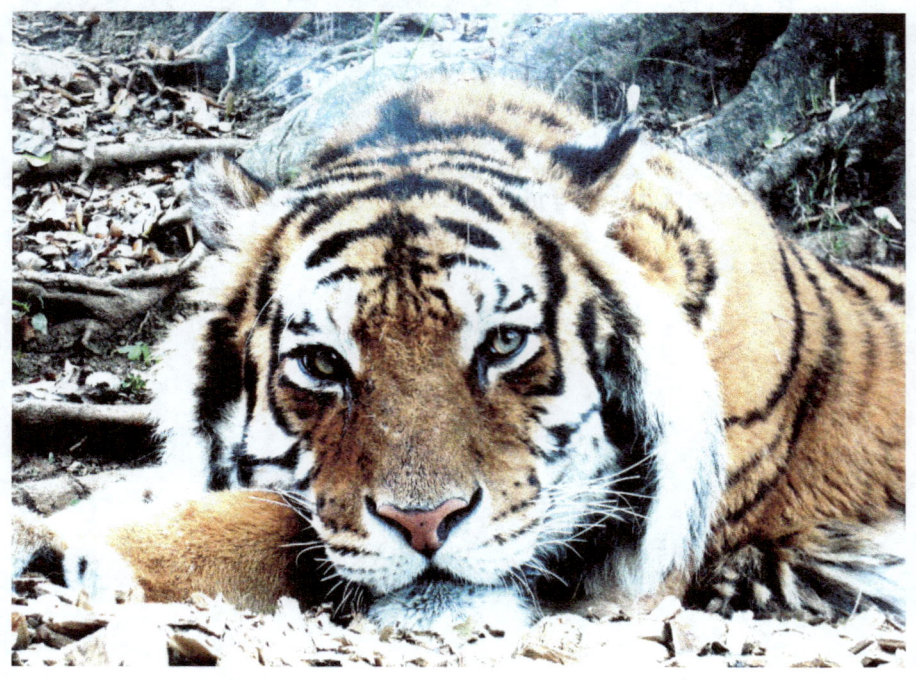

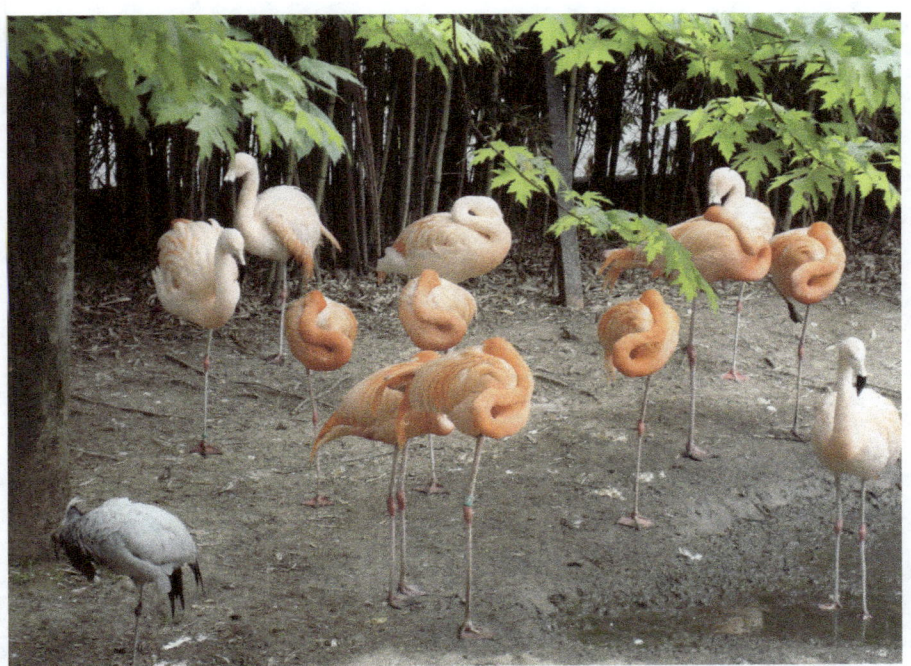

How sweet is love when it is sincere on both sides. It is a white heron in the snow: the eye does not separate them.

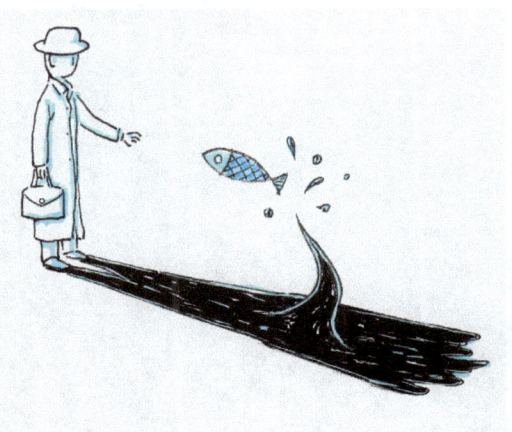

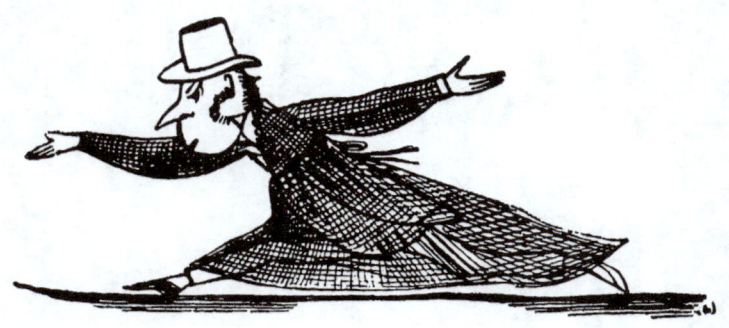

Empty your boat, make it lighter. Leave behind passions and hatreds and sail towards freedom.

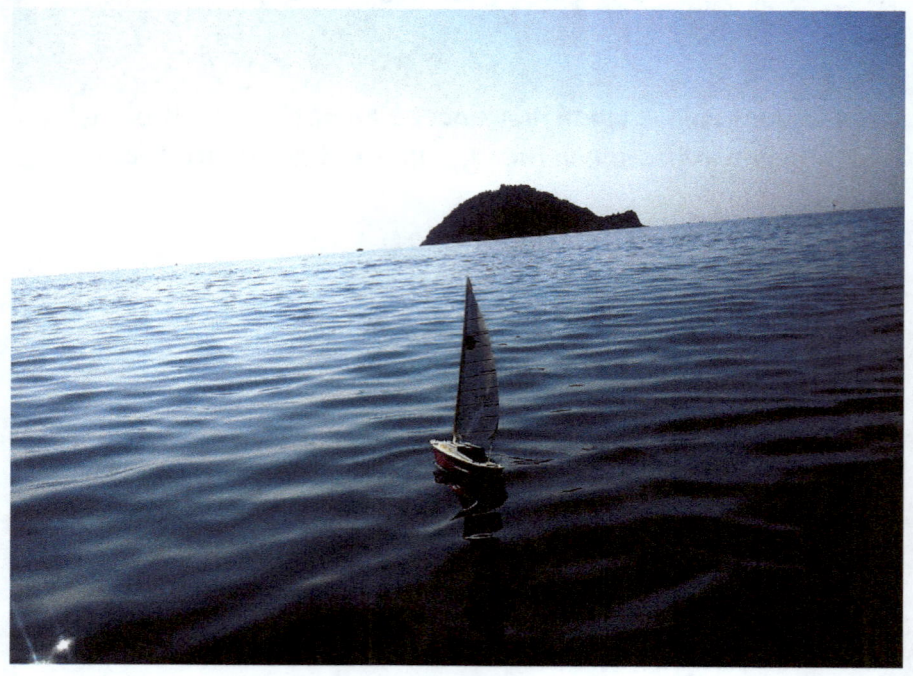

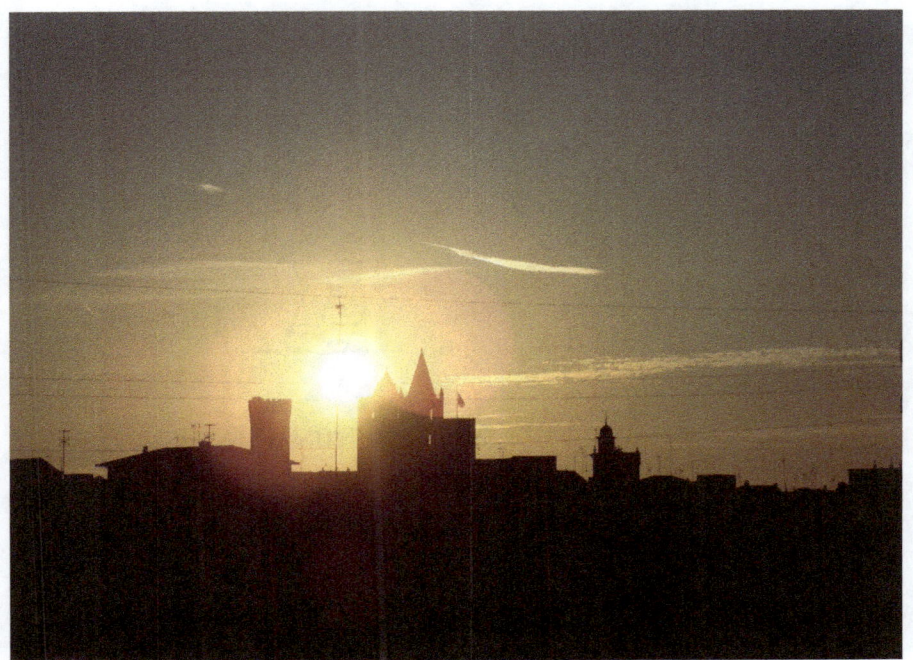

A ray of sunlight can change me.

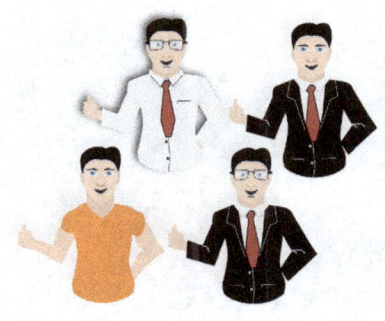

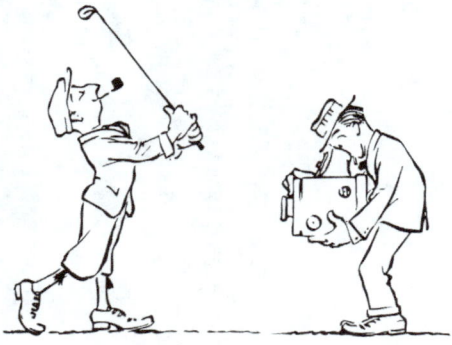

I prefer autumn to spring because in spring, you look at the earth, whereas in autumn, you look at the sky.

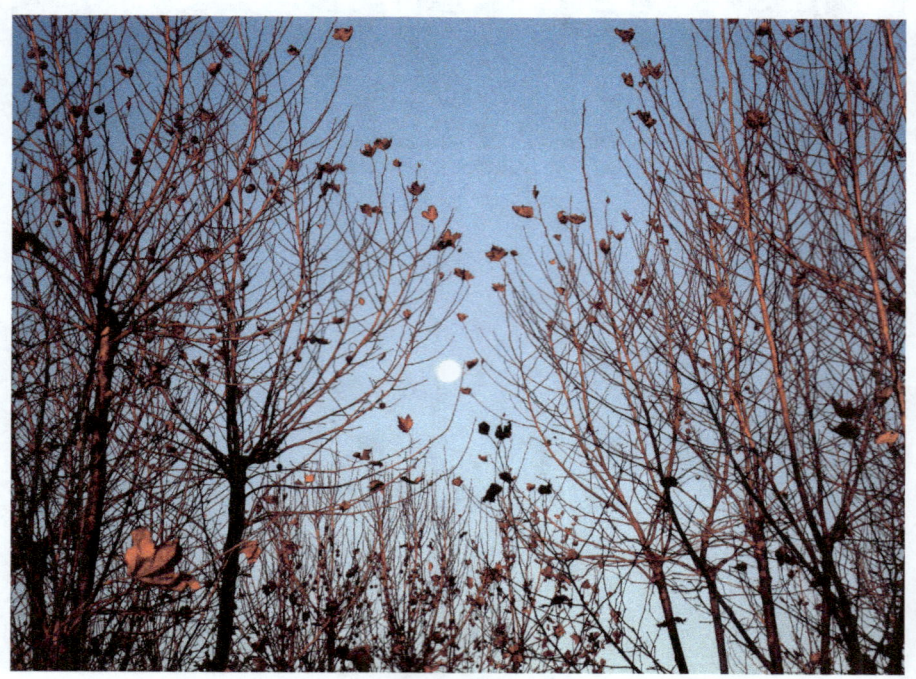

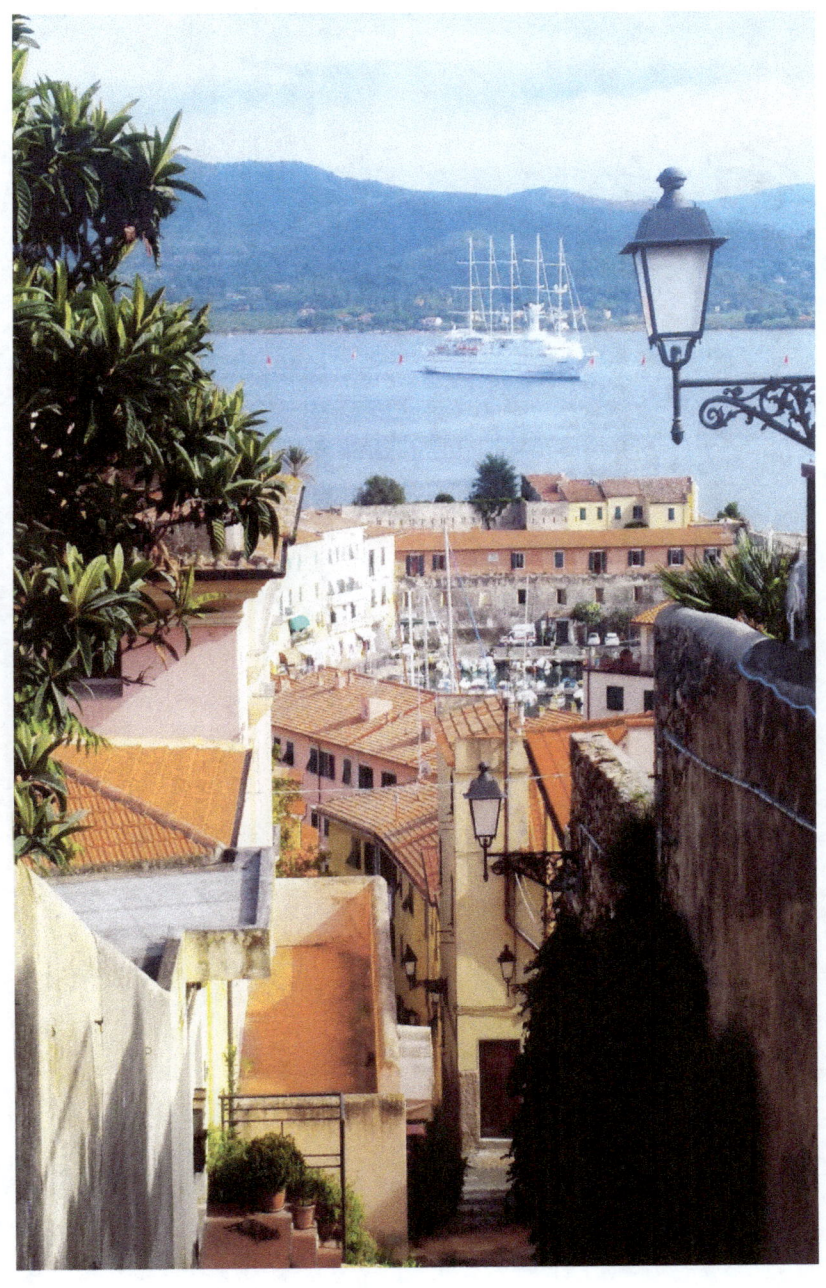

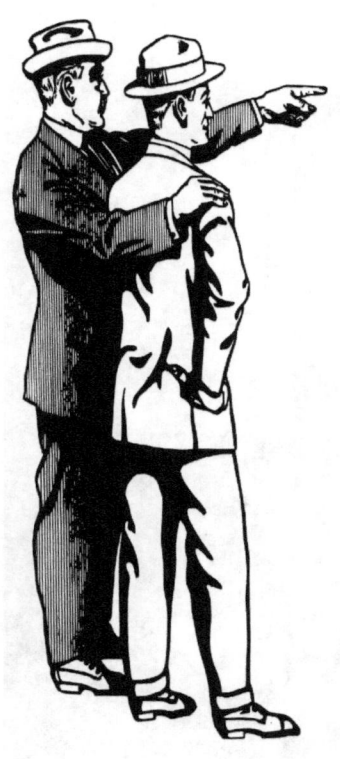

To reach port, you must sail.
To sail, avoid dropping anchor
and drifting.

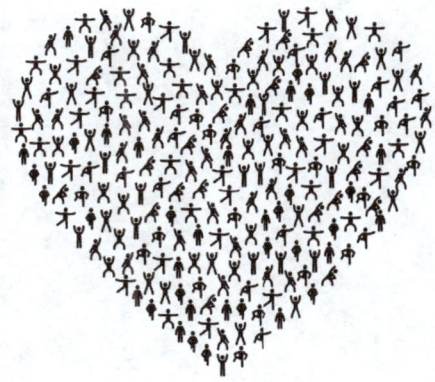

Everyone wants sunshine and maybe some shade.

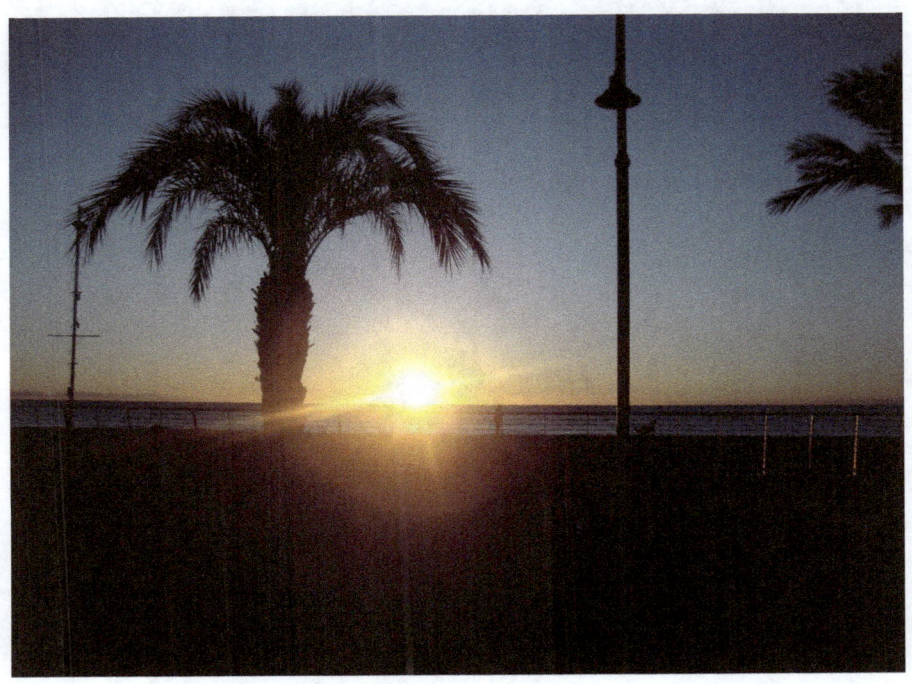

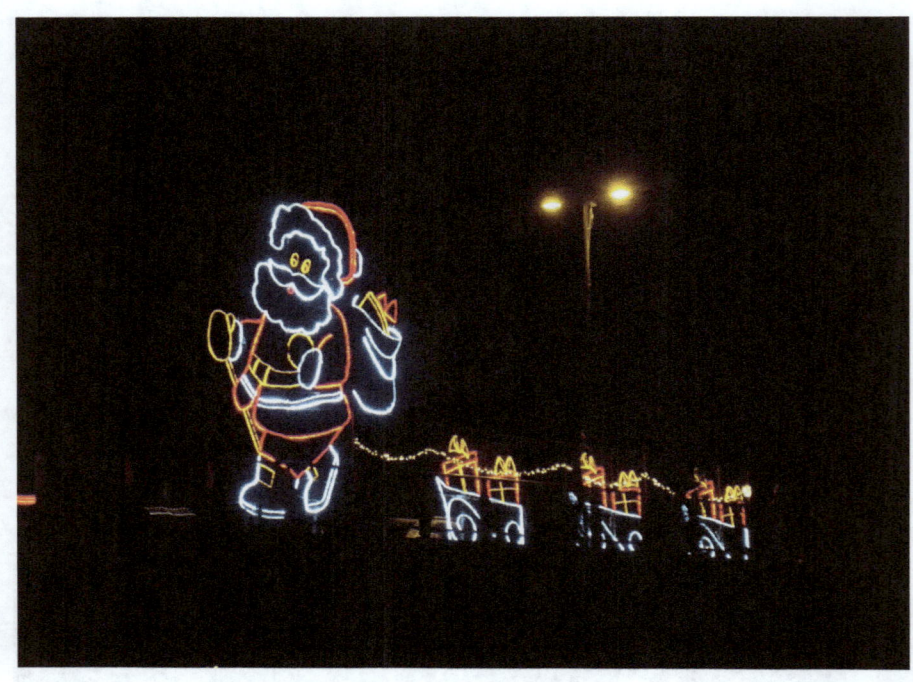

Adults don't believe in Santa Claus. They vote him.

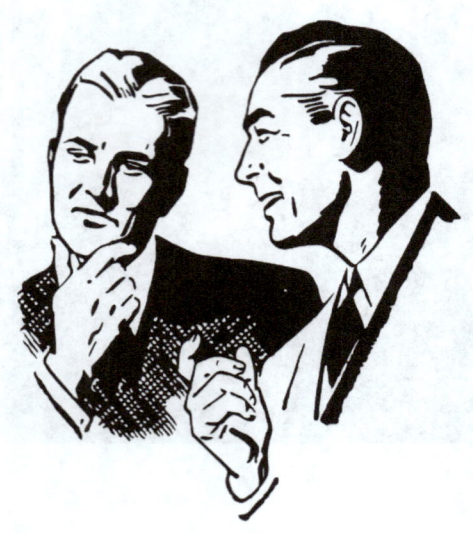

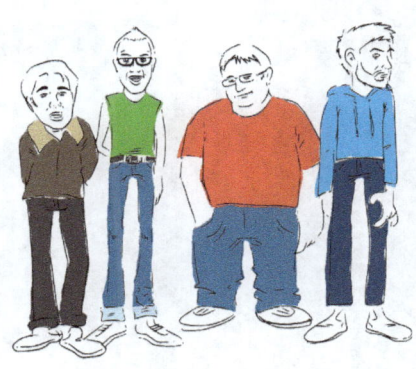

I will listen to your soul speaking,
as the shore listens to the waves' stories.

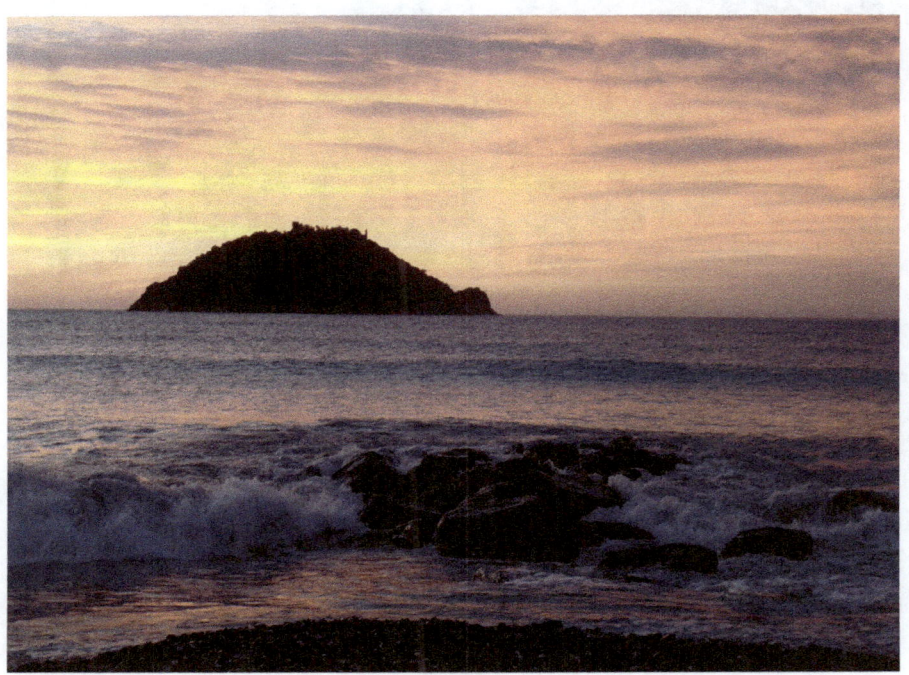

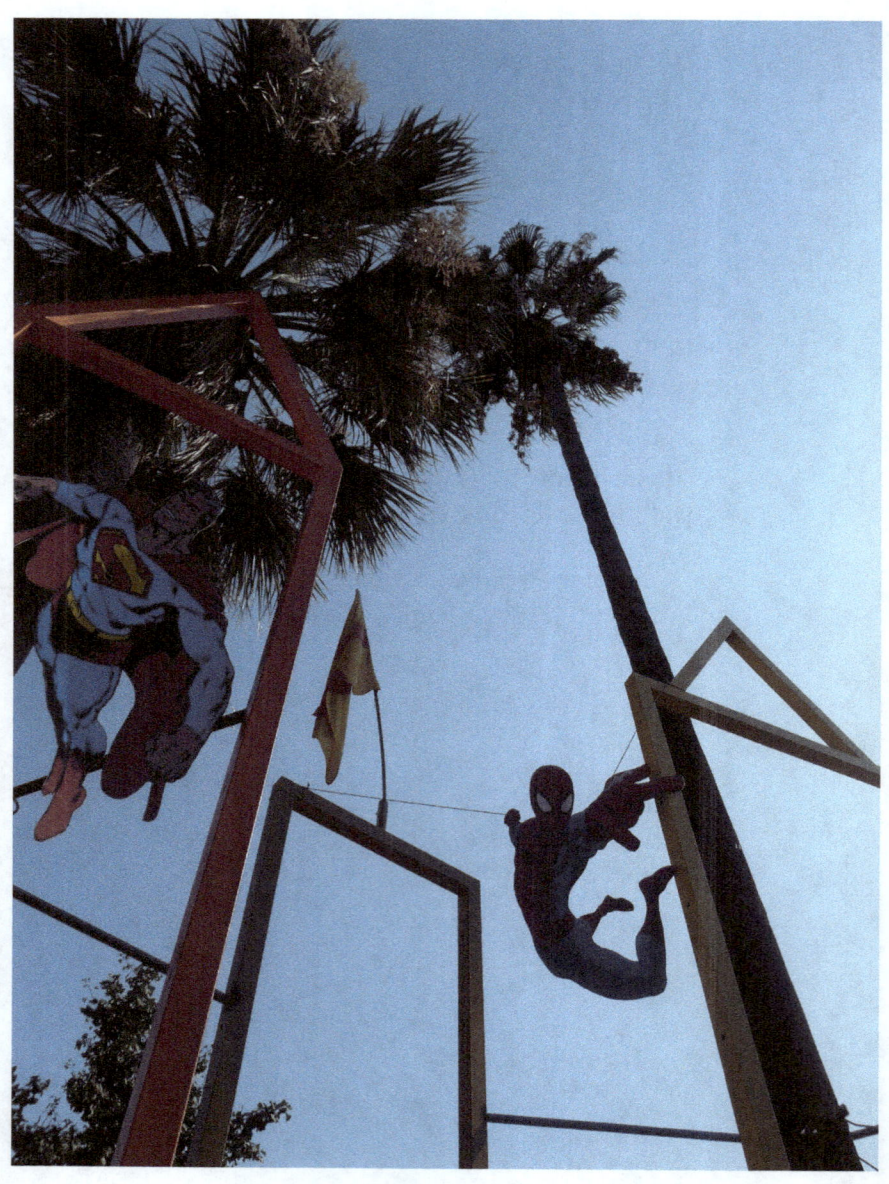

Seeing the world as it is and loving it
is the only heroism in the world.

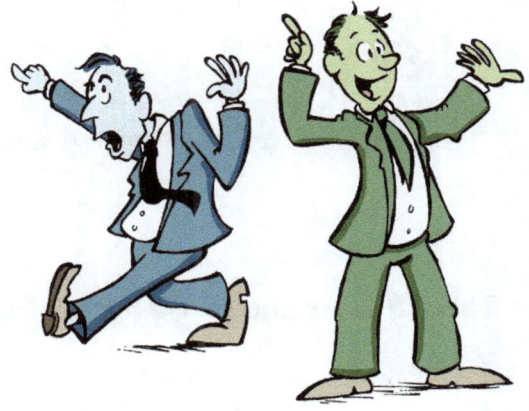

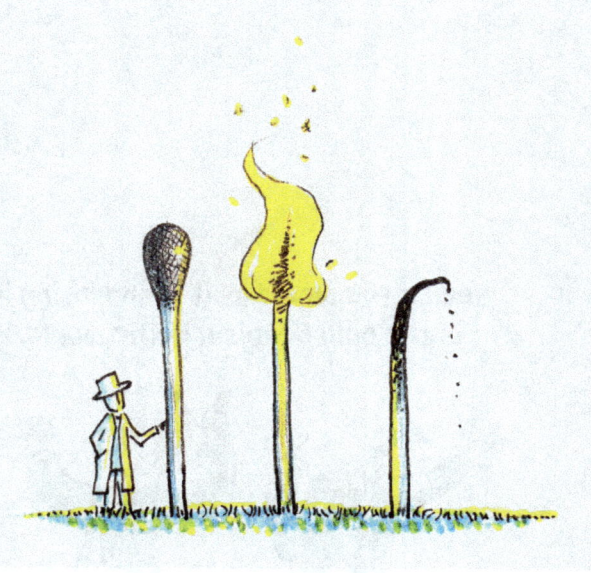

The sky is the eye's daily bread.

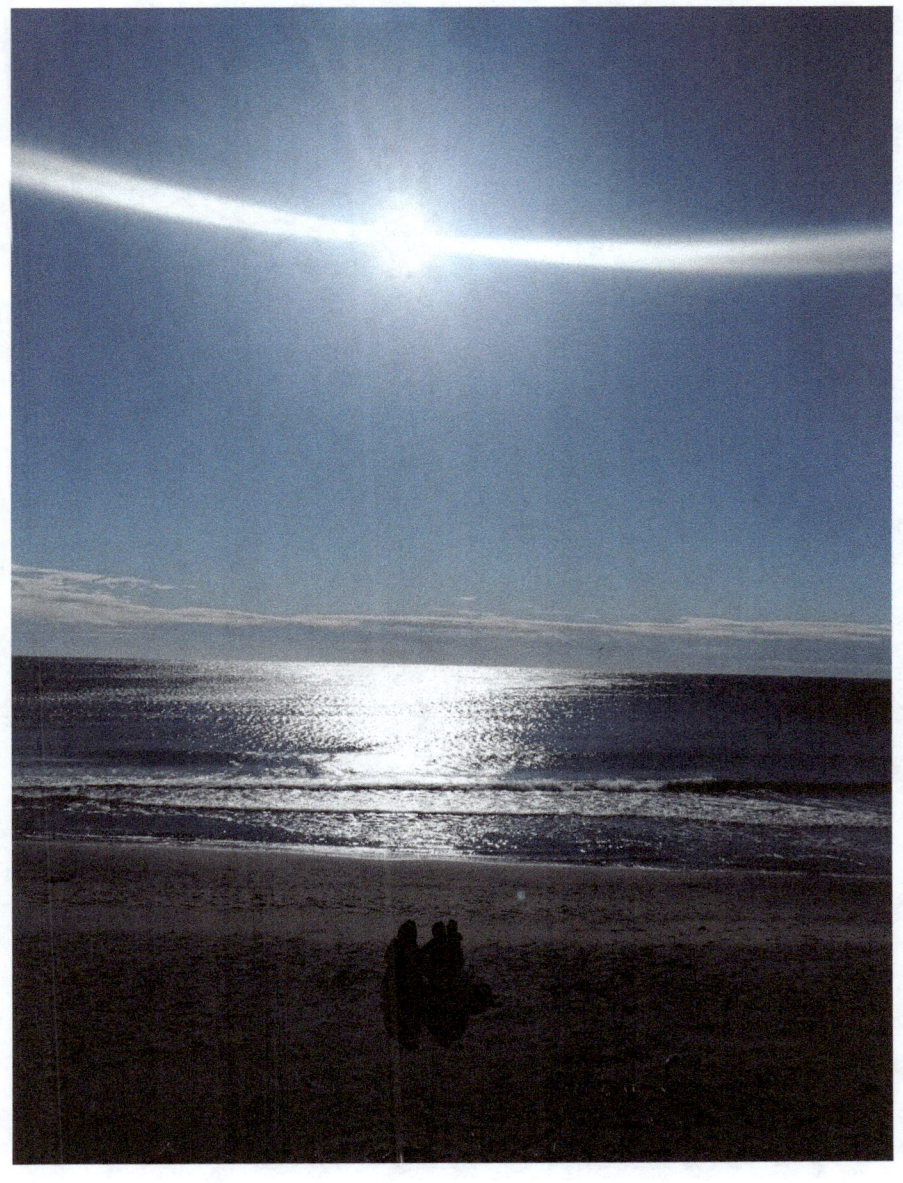

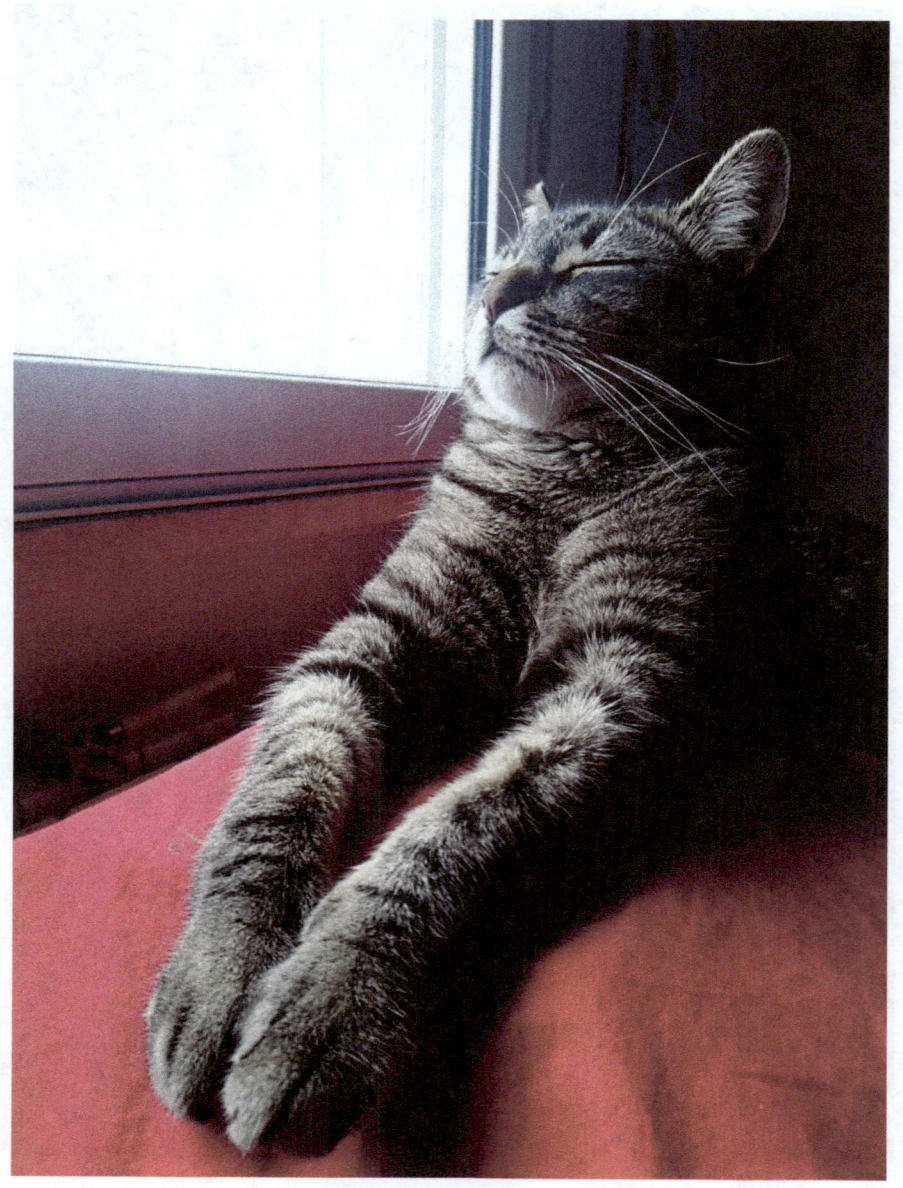

Intellectual cat wanted for hunting bookworms.

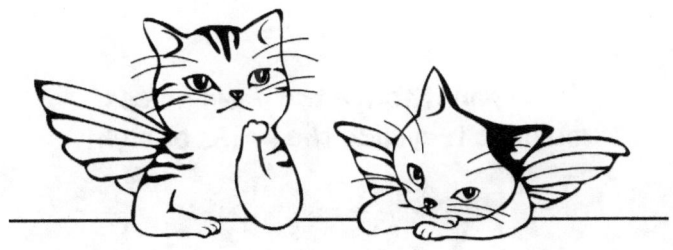

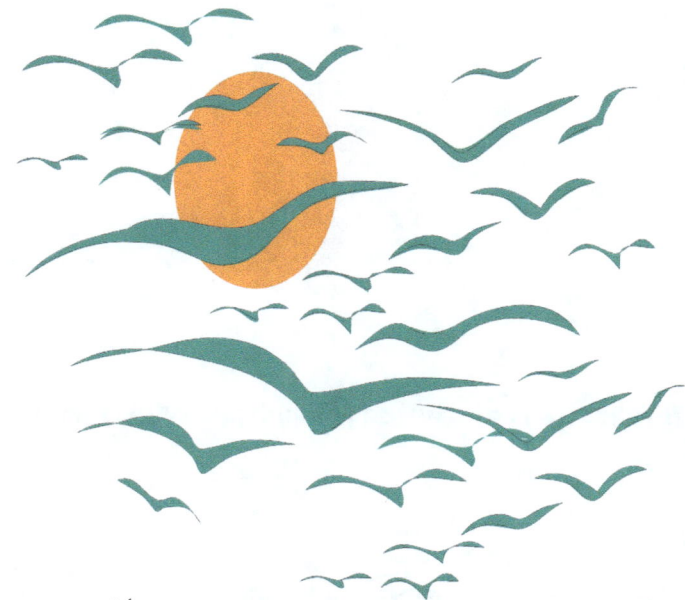

You cannot touch the dawn unless
you have travelled the paths of night.

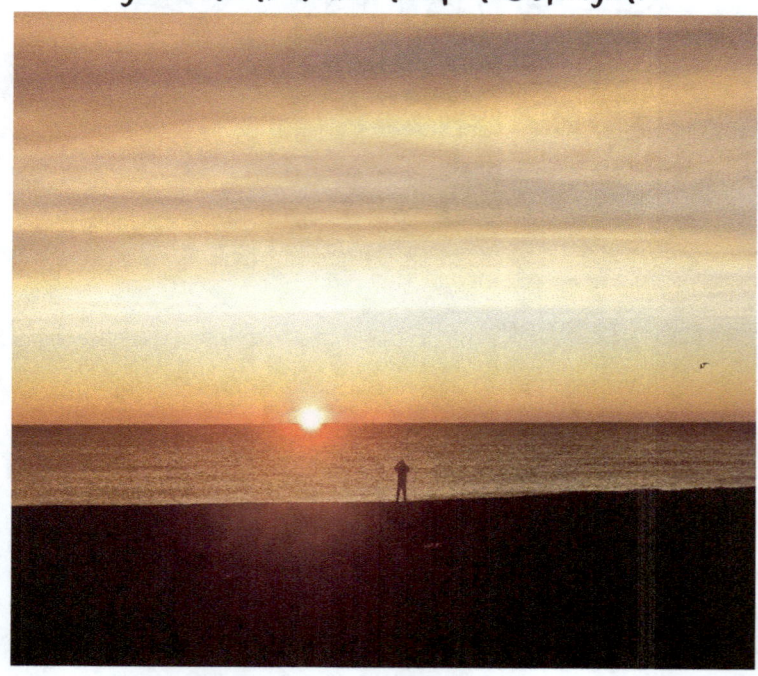

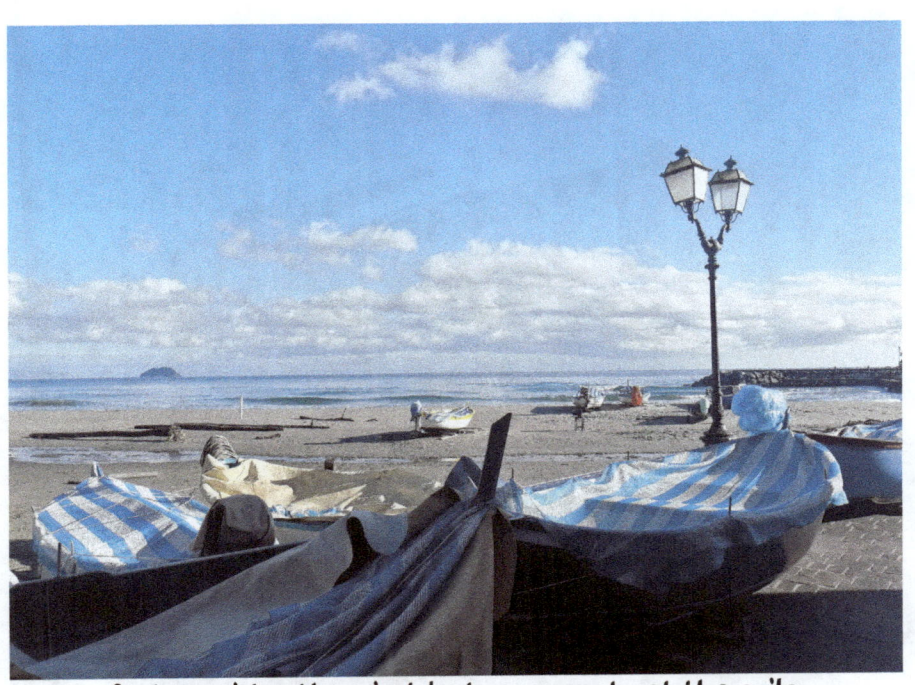

God provides the wind, but man must set the sails.

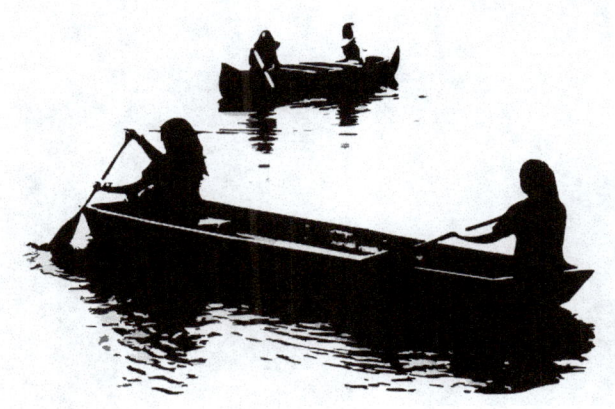

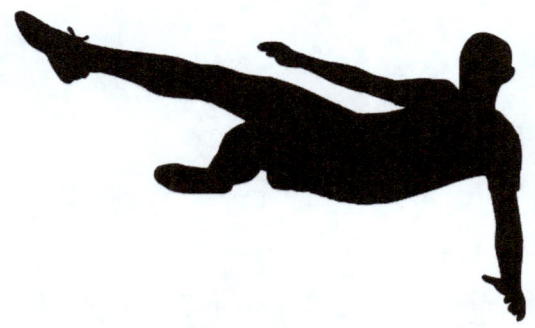

Playing football is easy but playing simple football is the hardest thing of all.

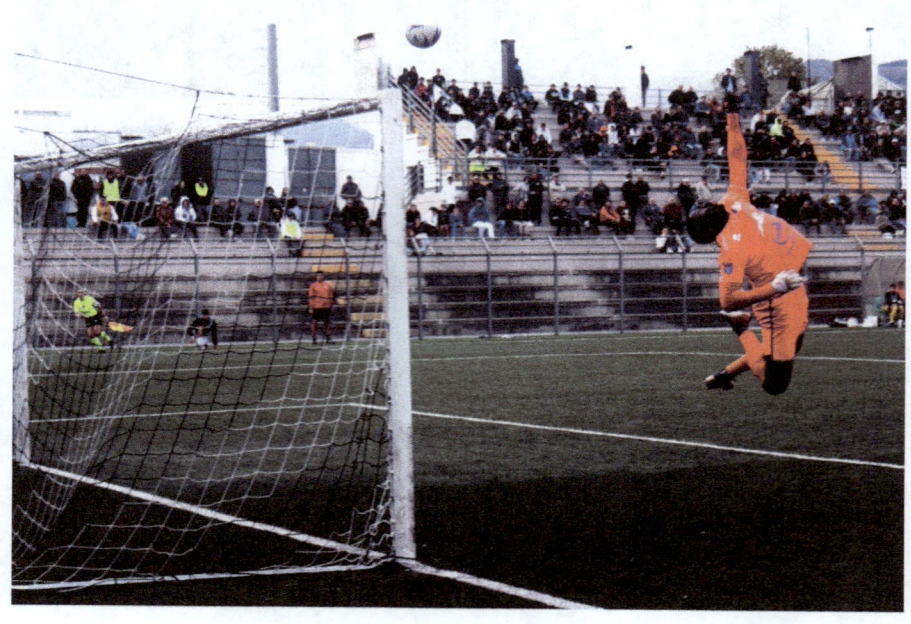

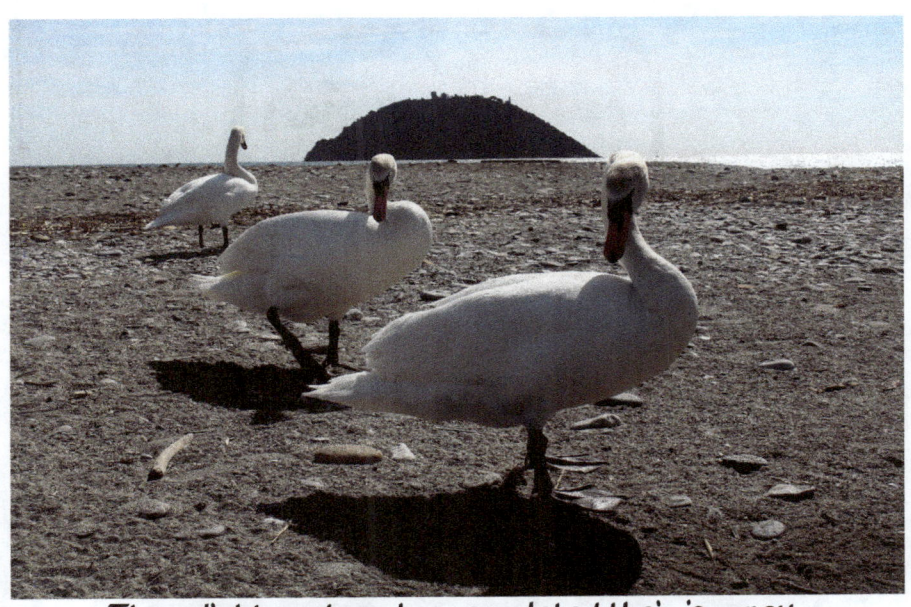

The enlightened one has completed their journey.
They have gone beyond suffering, broken all bonds,
and now live in complete freedom. They do not dwell anywhere
but constantly take flight, like swans leaving their lake.

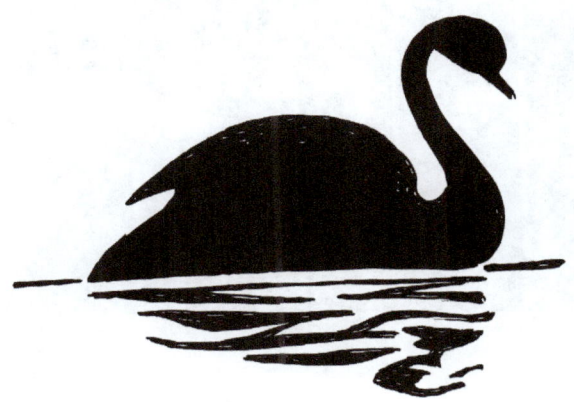

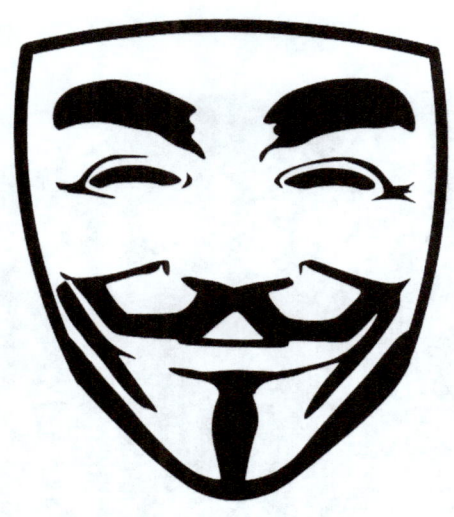

Sometimes, the mask falls, revealing a person's true nature.

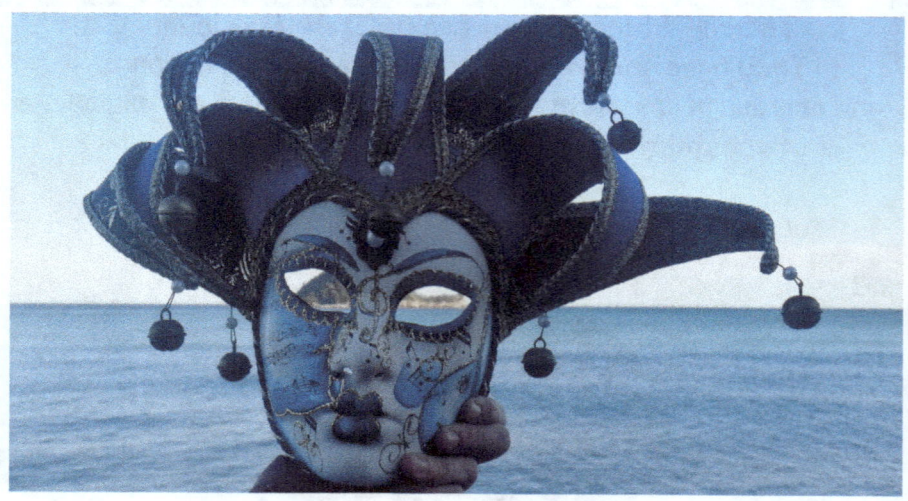

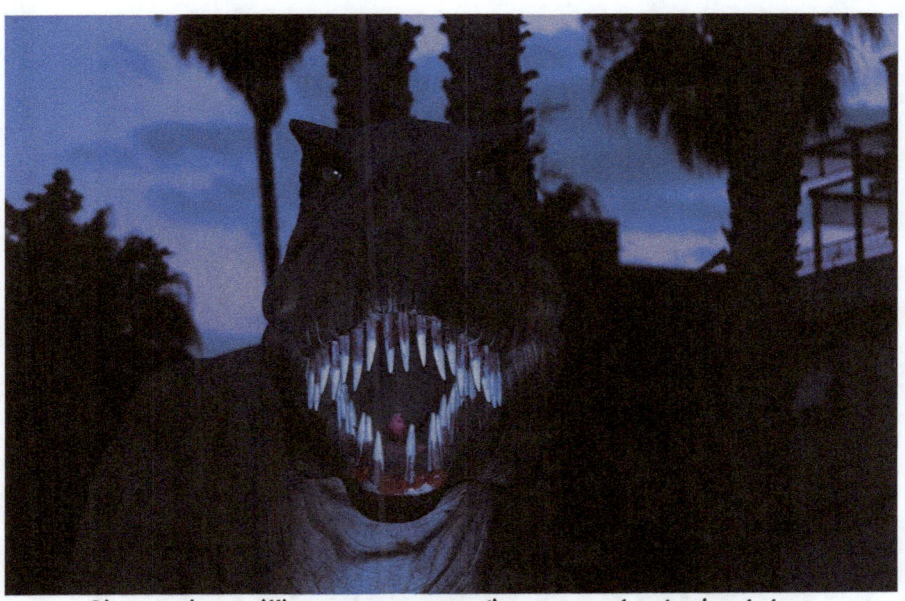

Sixty-five million years ago dinosaurs had a bad day.

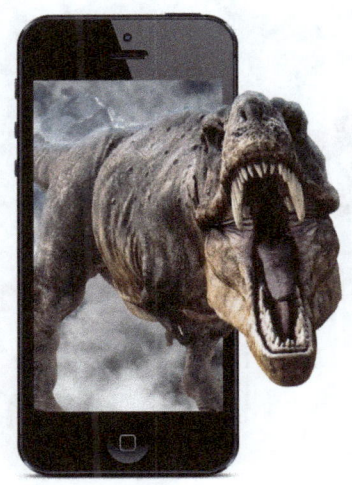

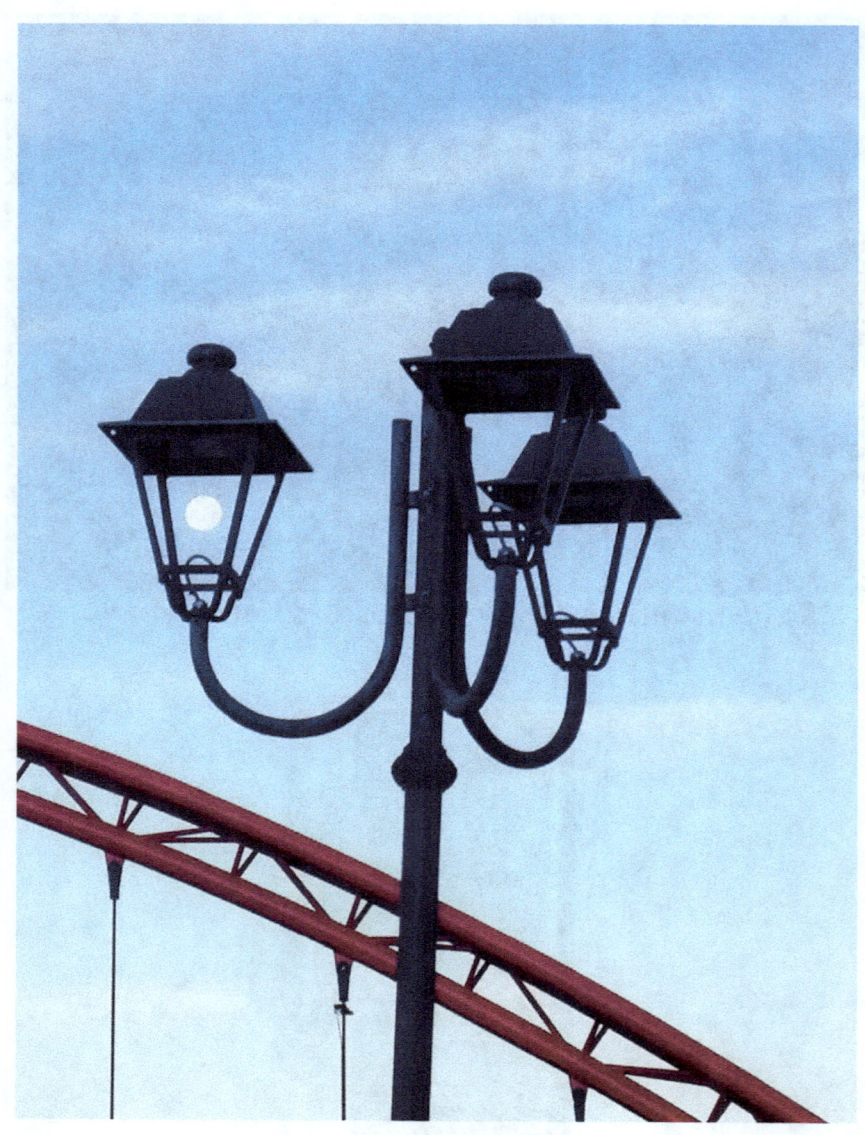

There is no need for streetlamps in the Way of Love;
there, everything is already bright!

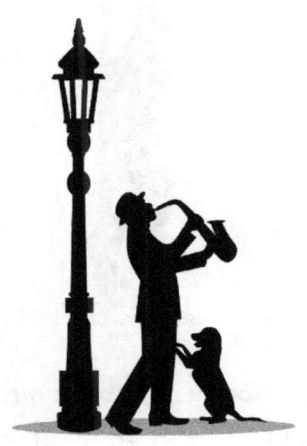

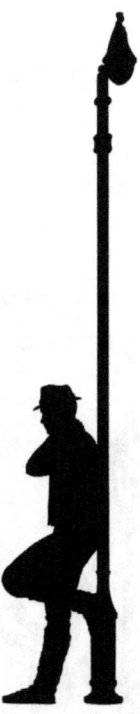

Semaforo. Lampione pubblico molto timido: arrossisce non appena ci si avvicina.

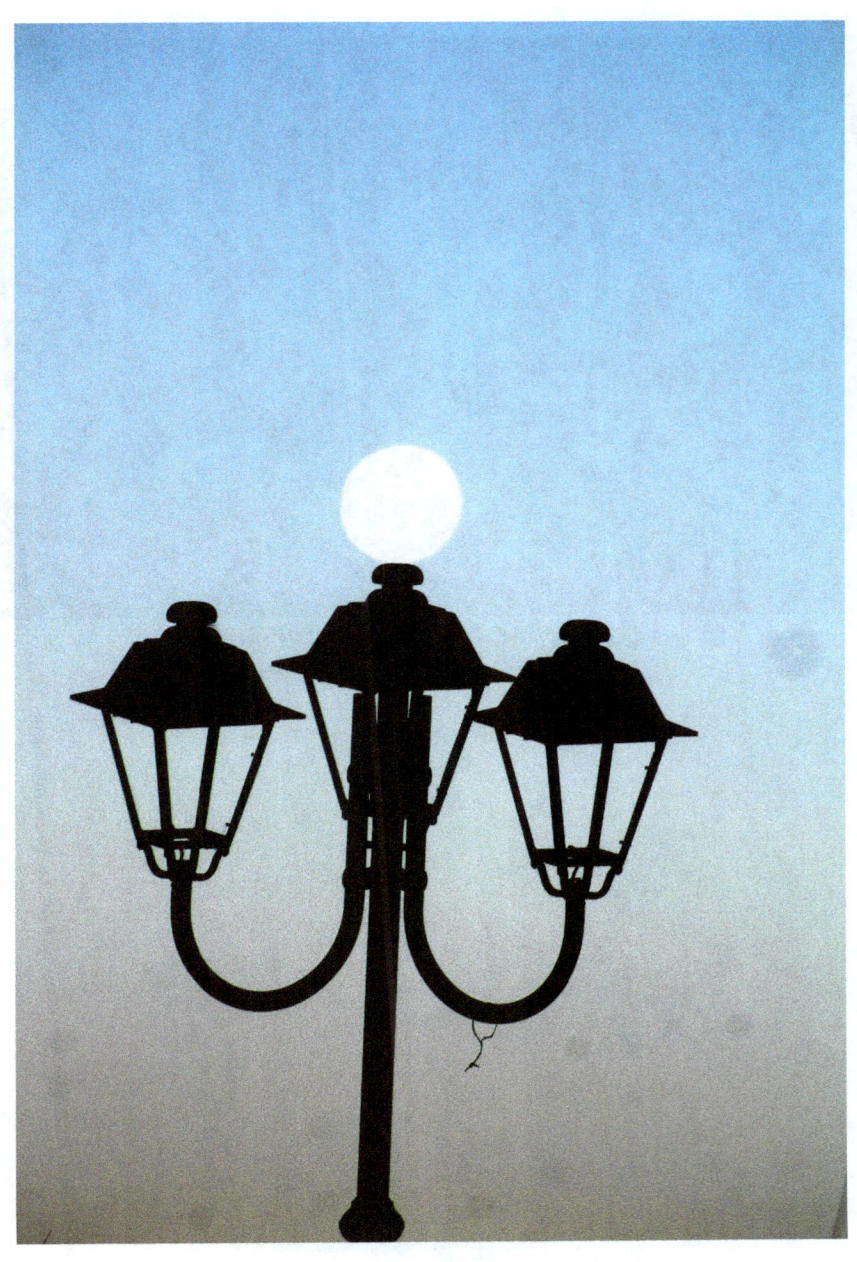

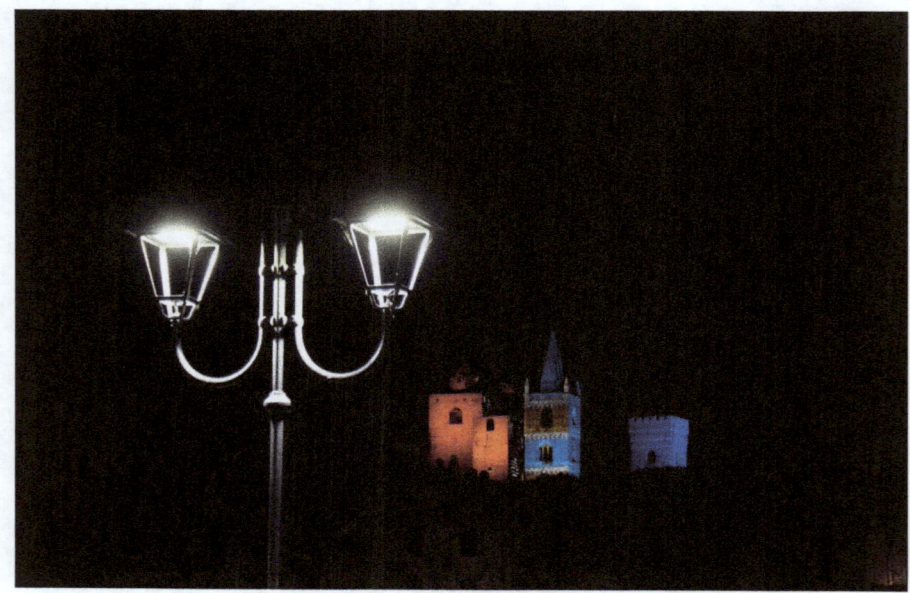

Life is tragedy in the foreground,
but comedy in the background.

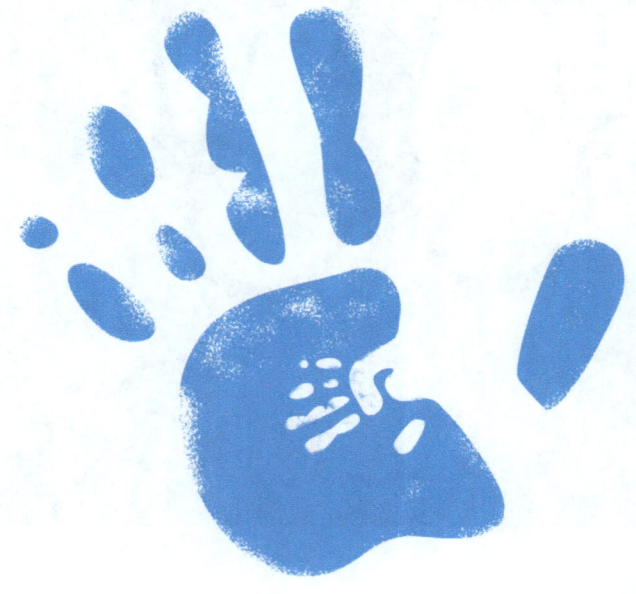

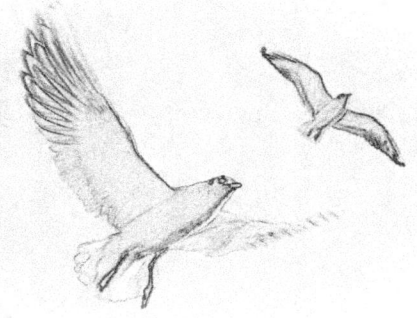

Poetry is the expression of the sea in a glass.

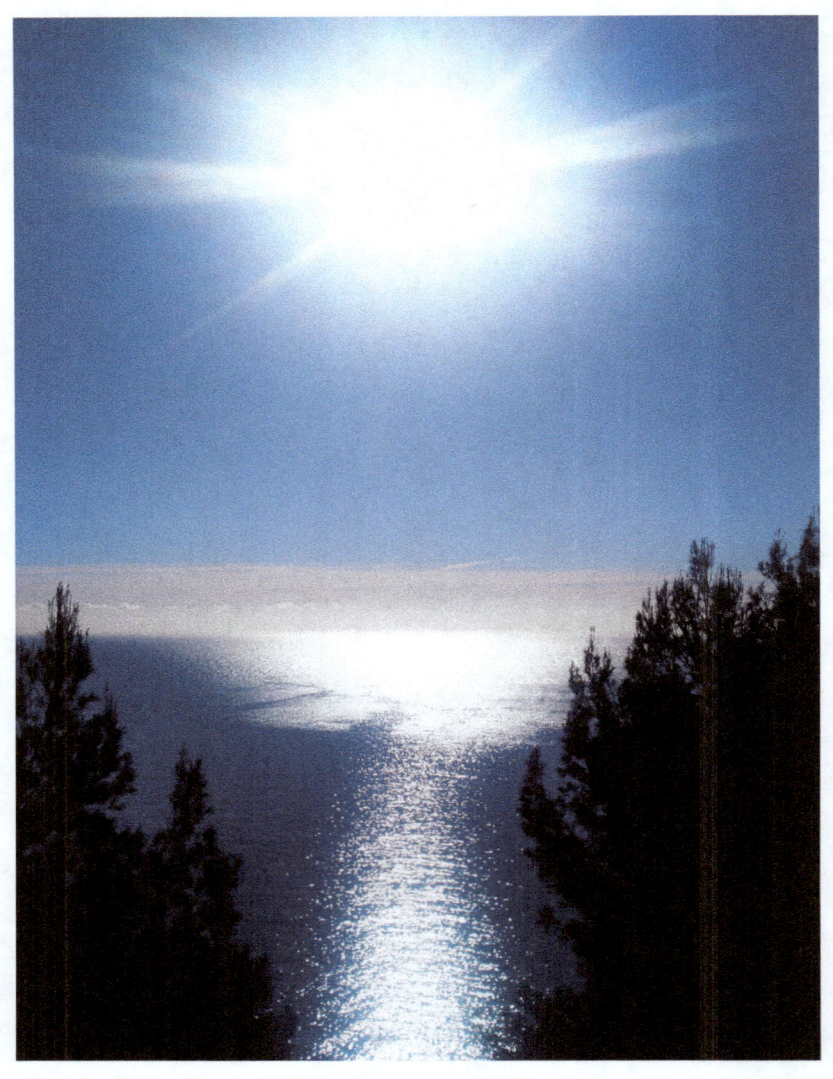

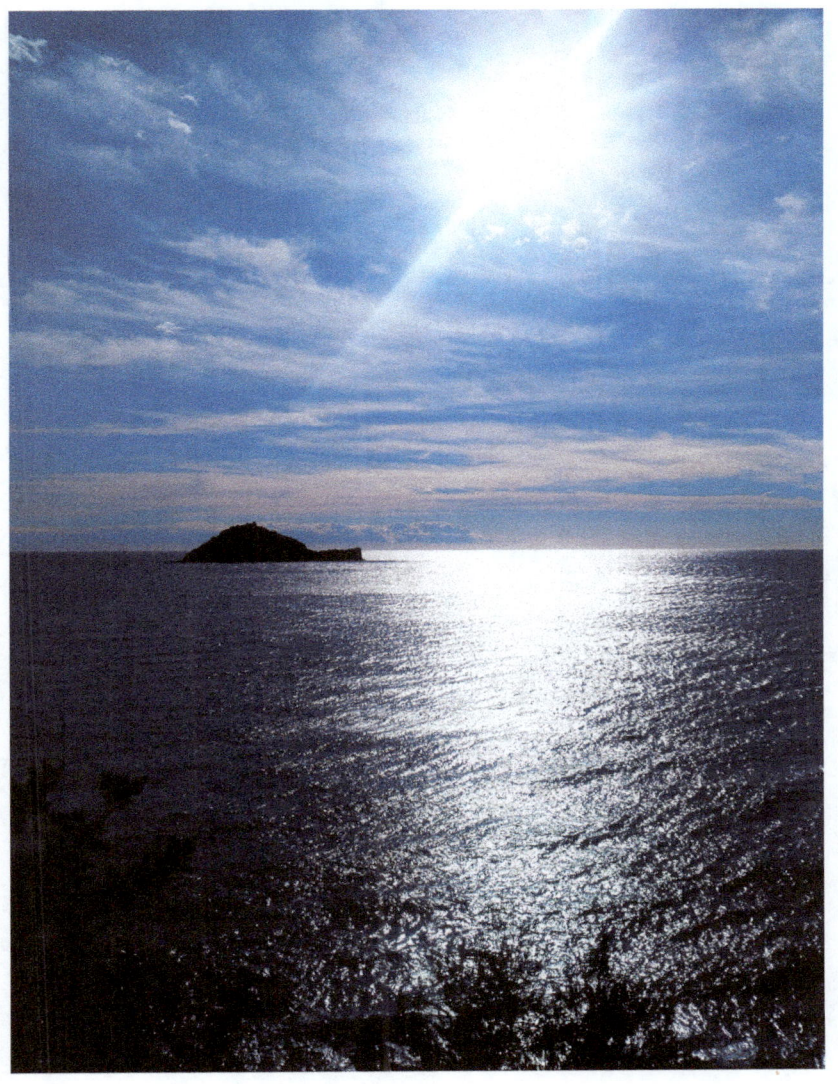

The tongue is not enough to tell
and the hand to write all the sea's wonders.

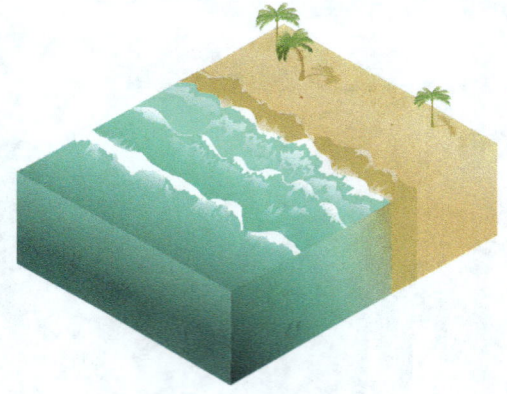

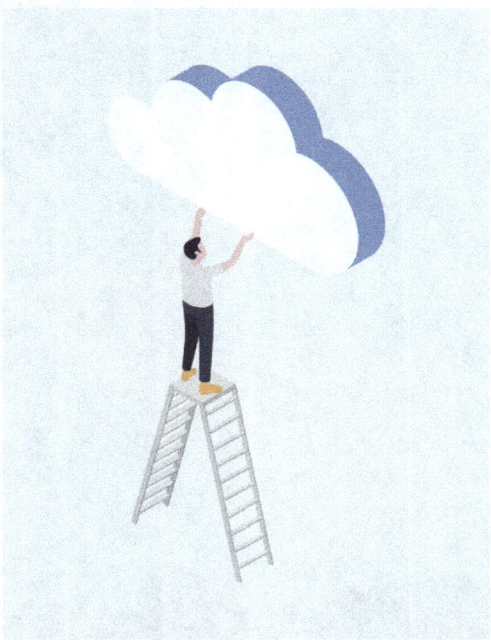

You don't have to travel around the world
to understand that the sky is blue everywhere.

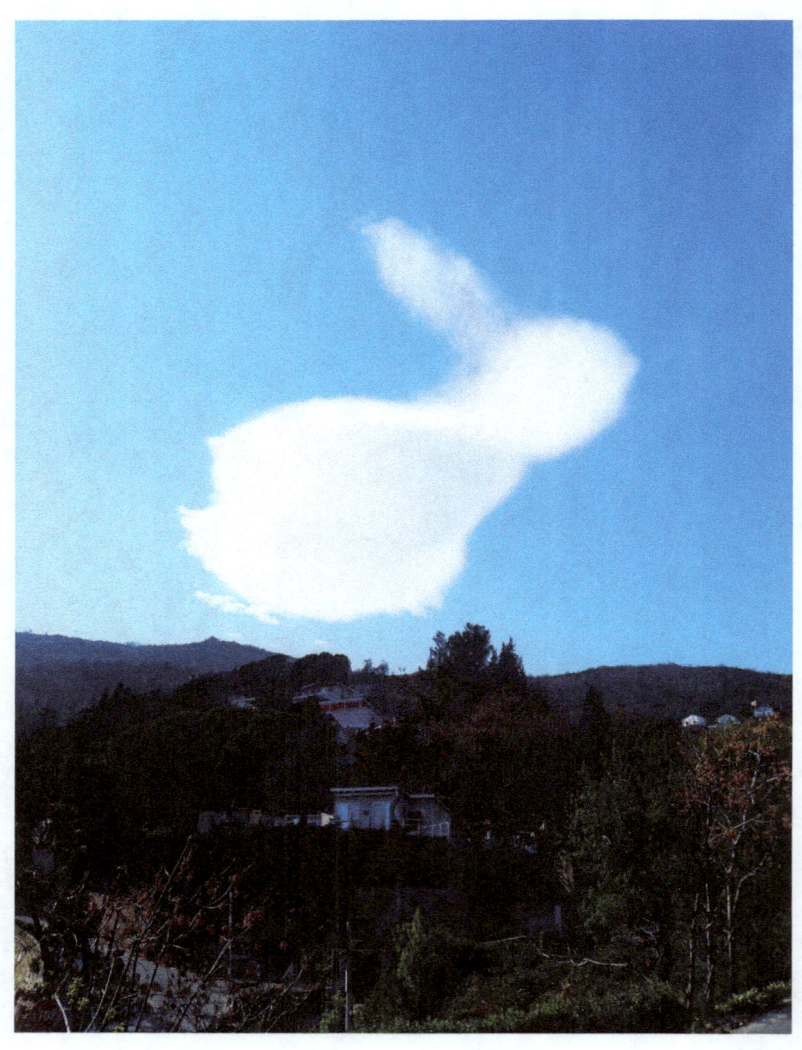

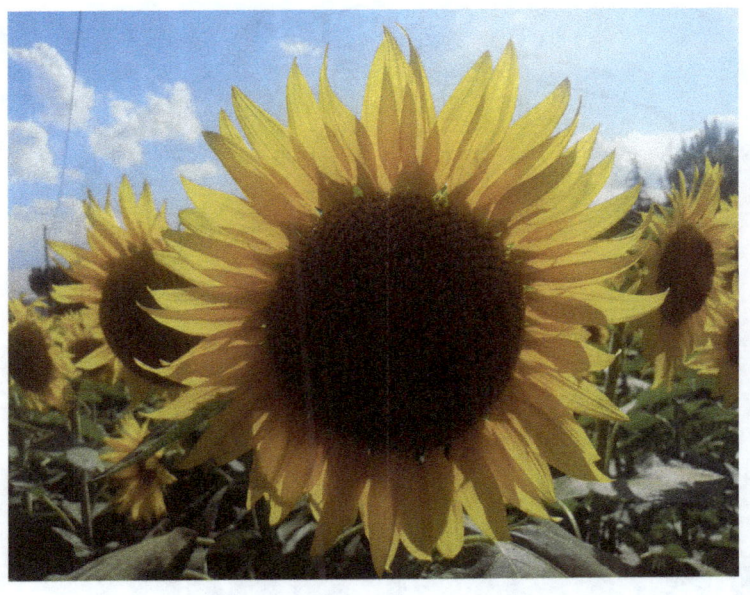

My model in life is the sunflower
because I always seek light and truth.

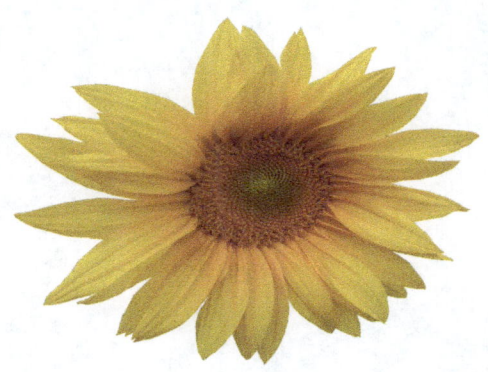

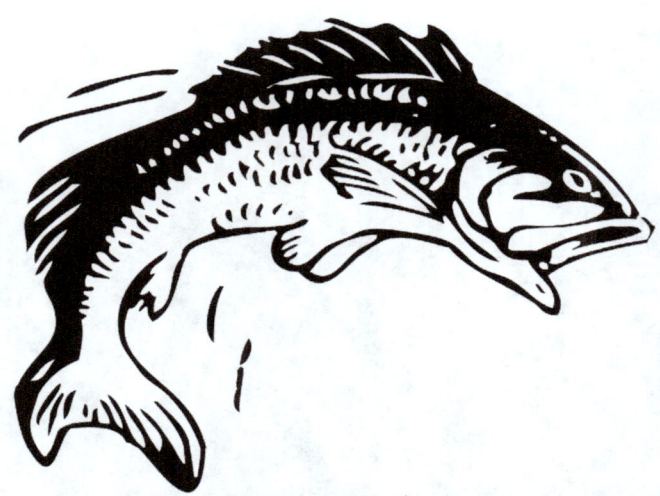

I will listen to your soul's language
as the beach listens to the waves' story.

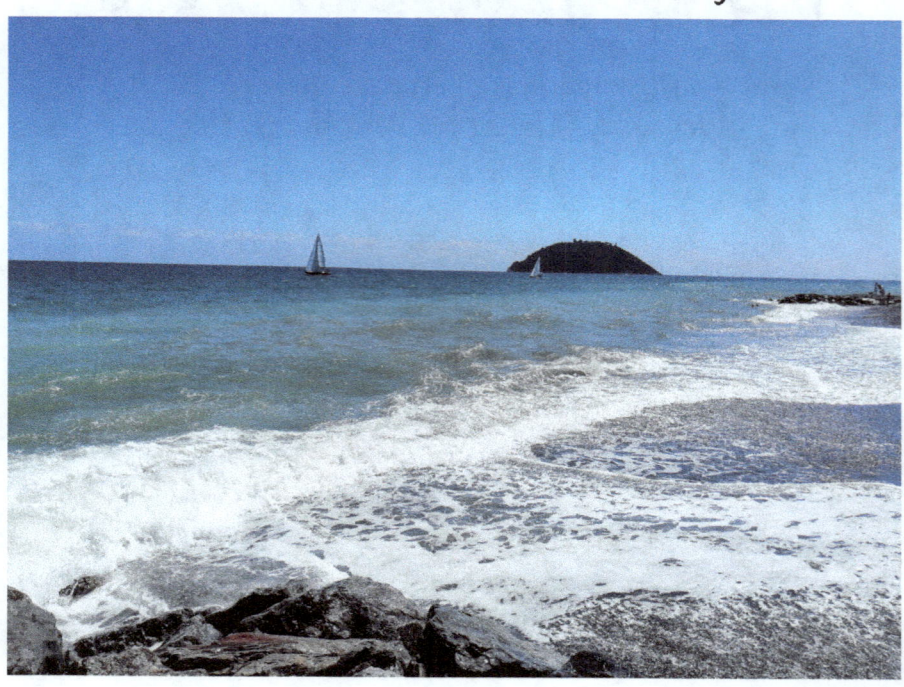

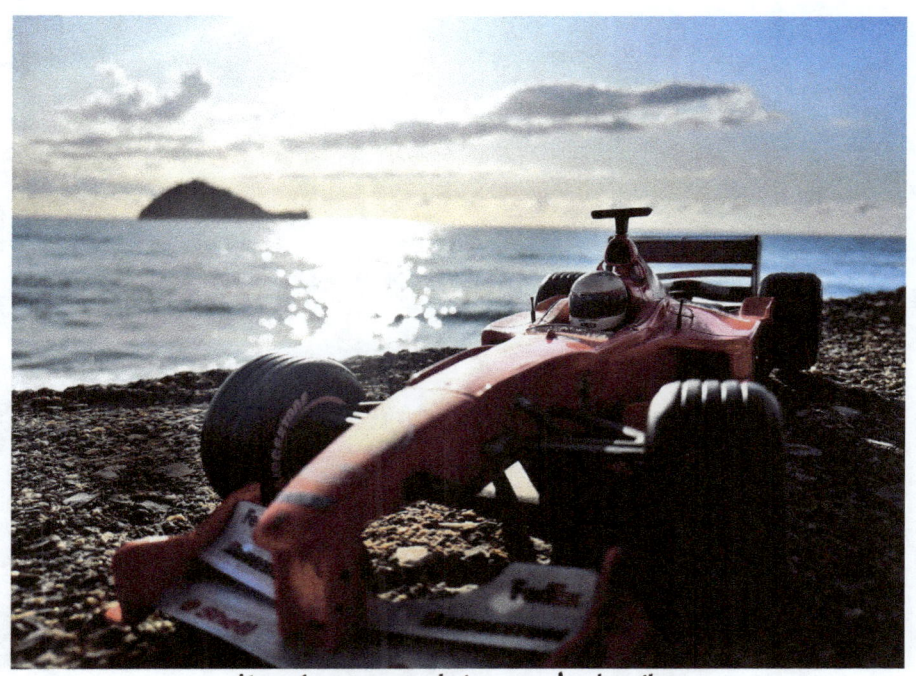

He who comes late, parks badly.

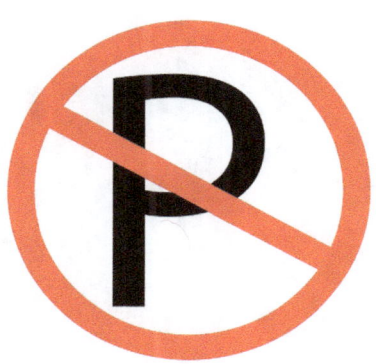

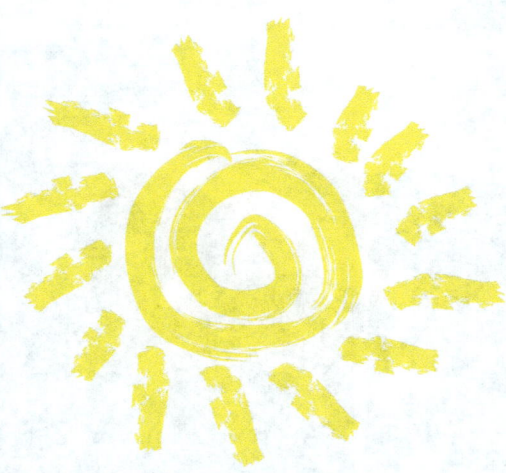

For the sailor who does not know where to land,
no wind is favourable.

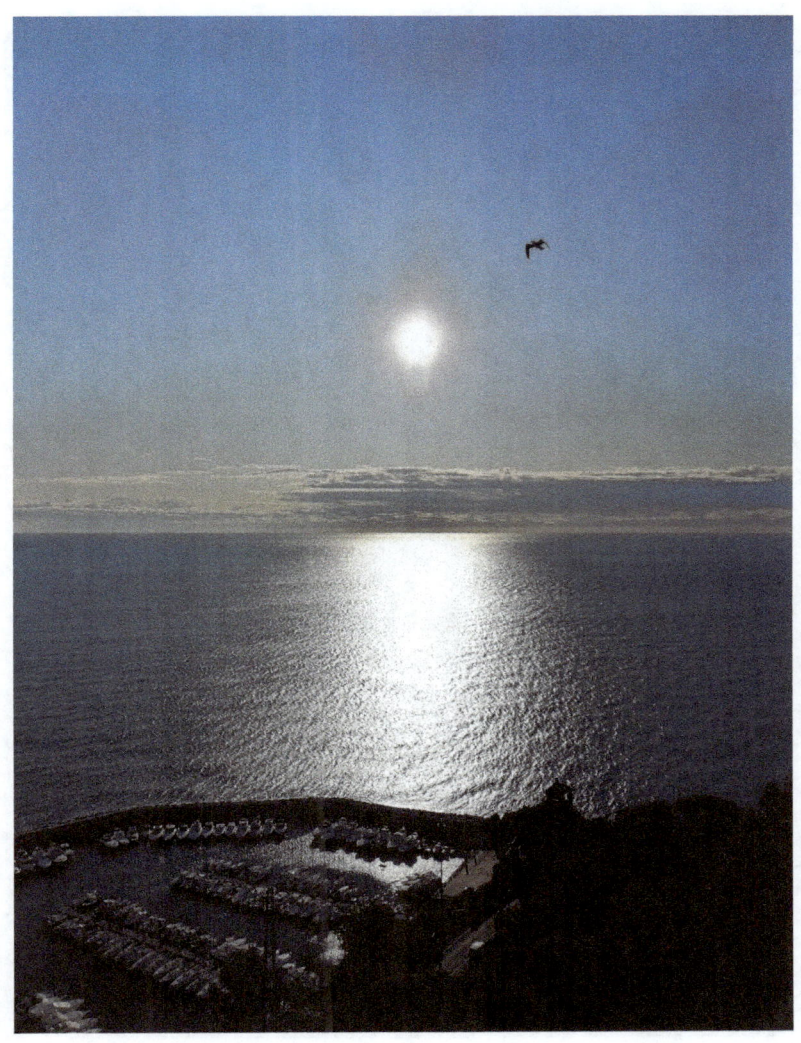

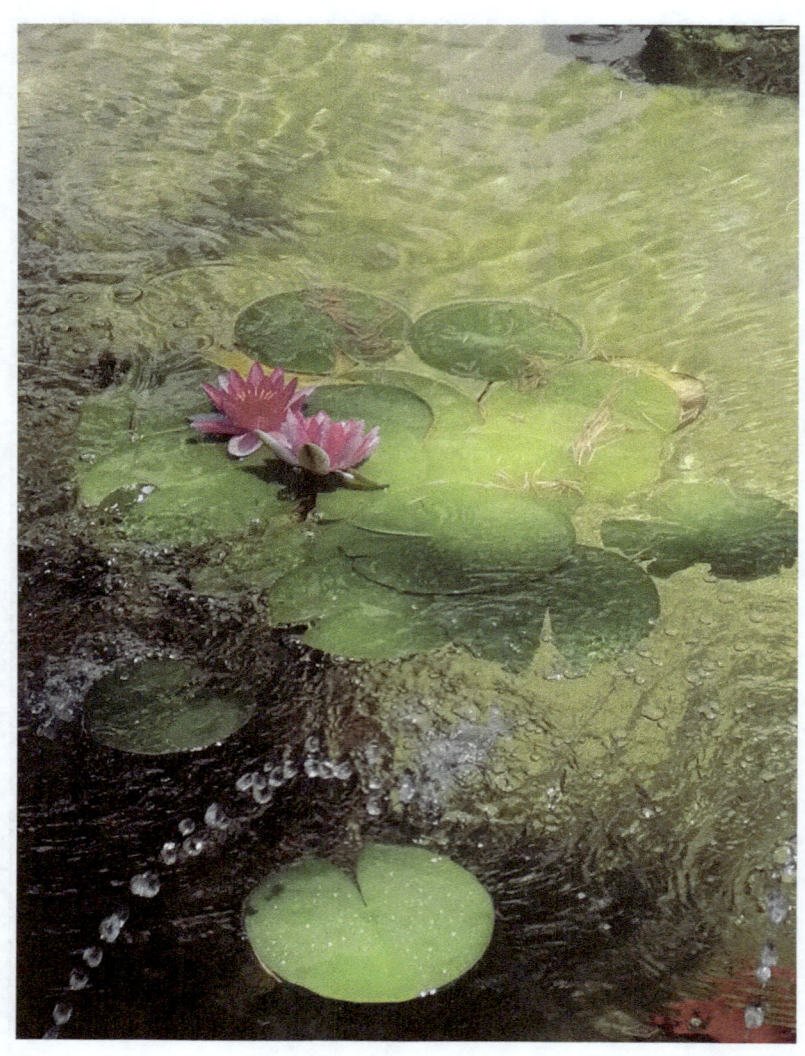

A woman's heart is as fleeting as a drop of water on a lotus leaf.

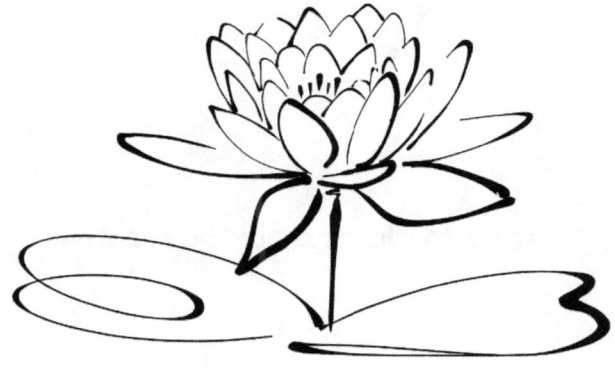

56

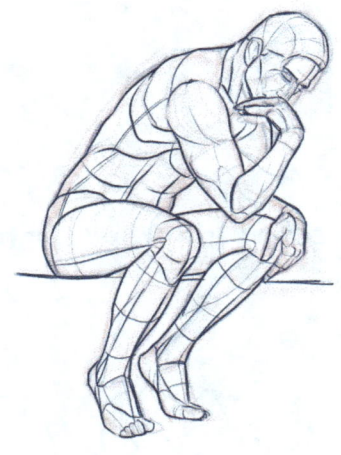

Statues to silence should be erected.

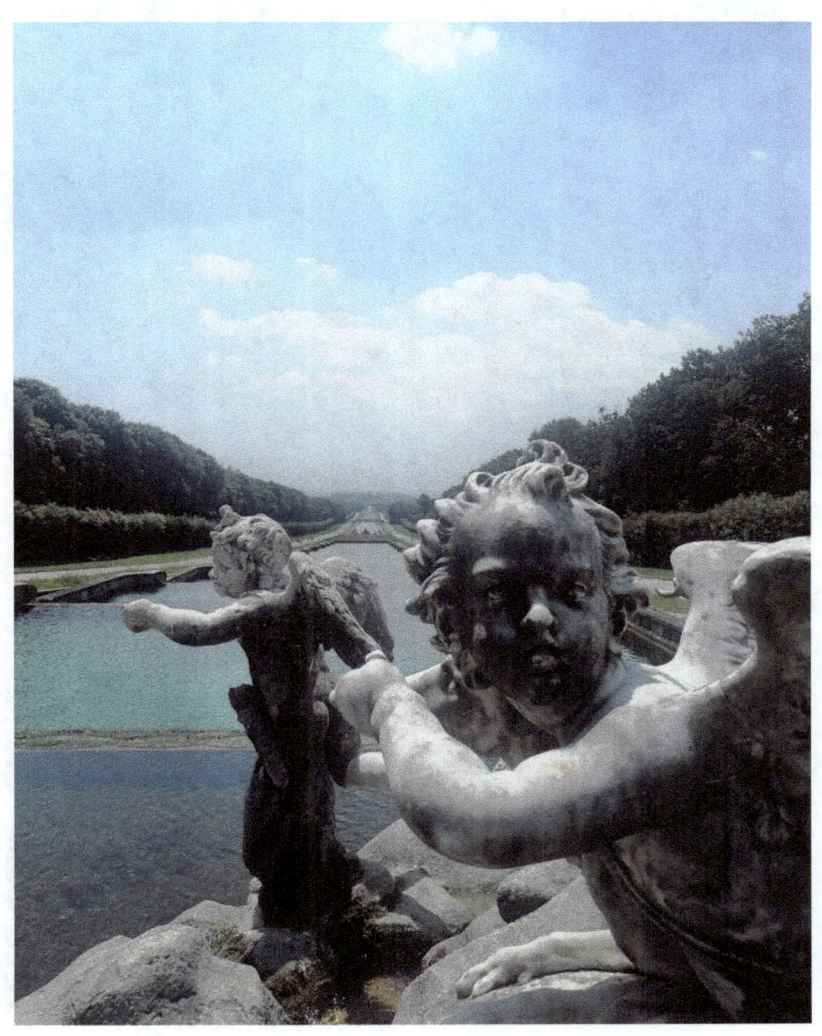

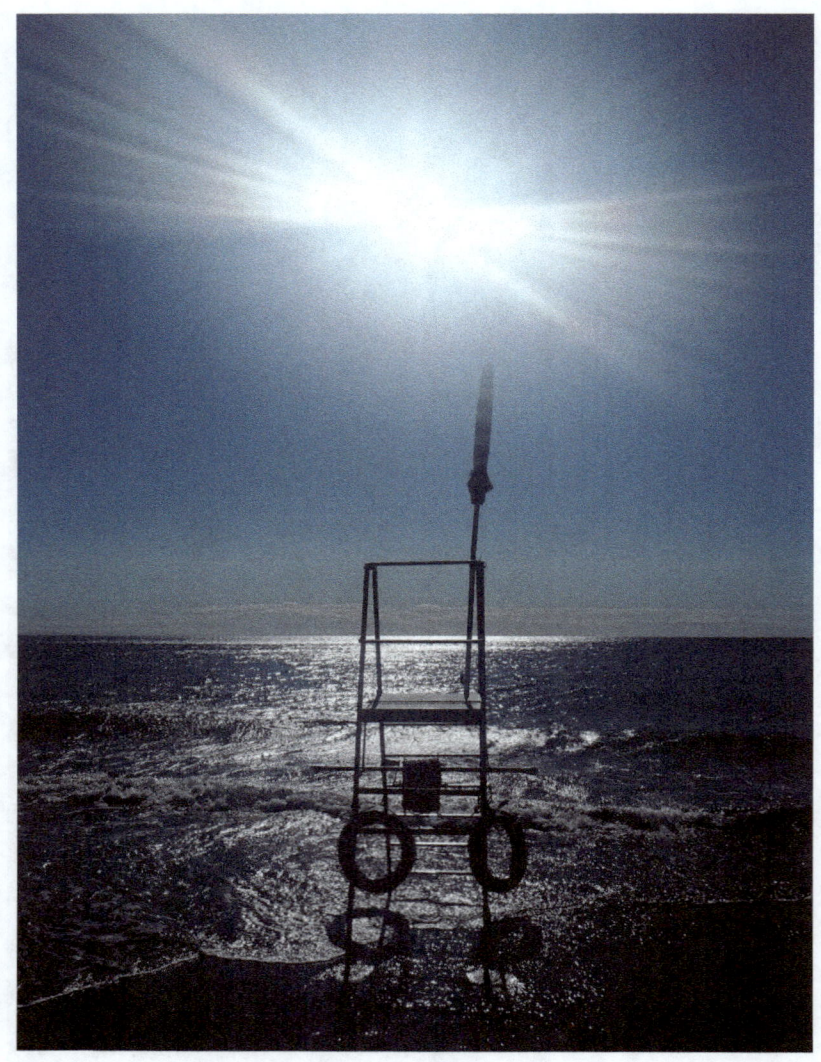

Hold on to people with the sea inside,
but it's okay if they have the pool outside...

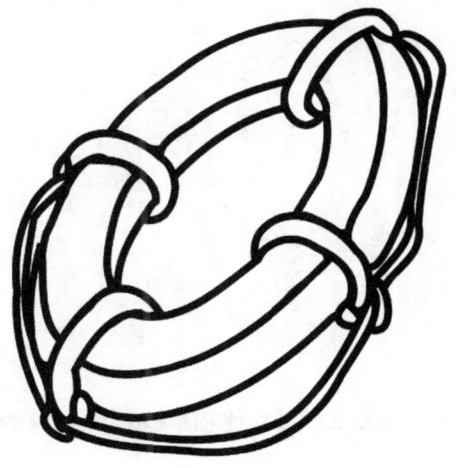

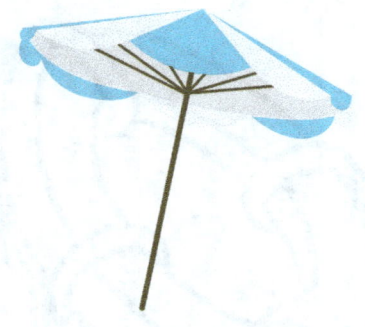

If paradise exists, it surely has a beach.

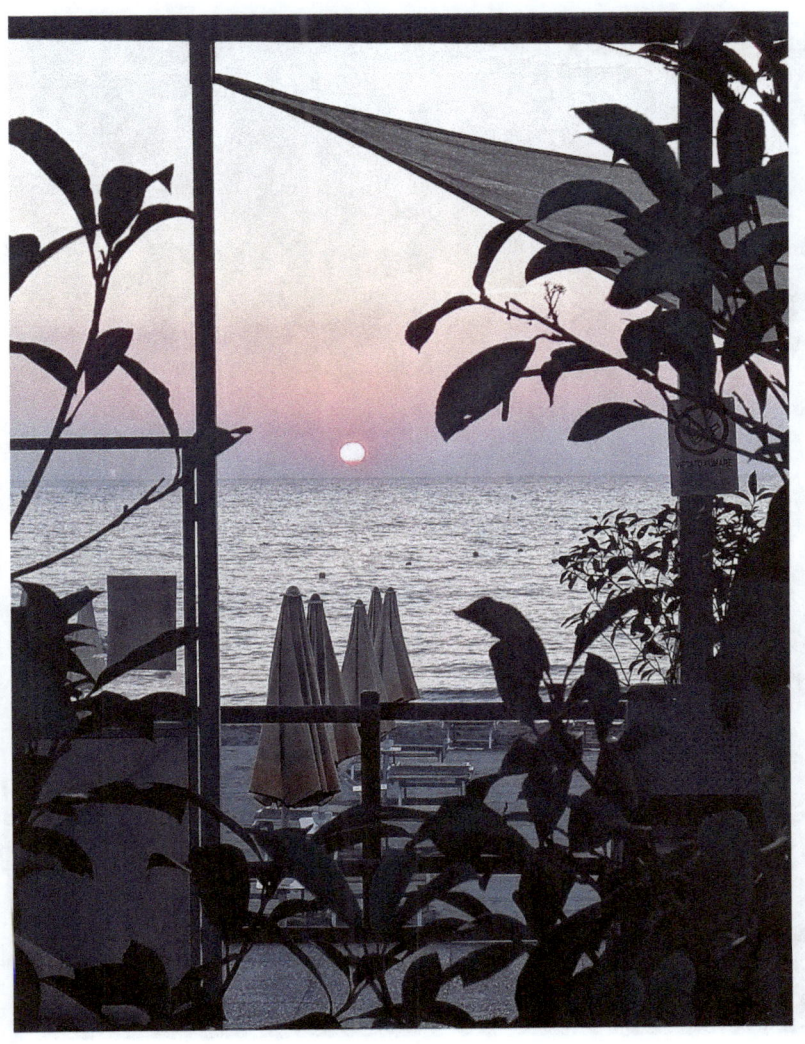

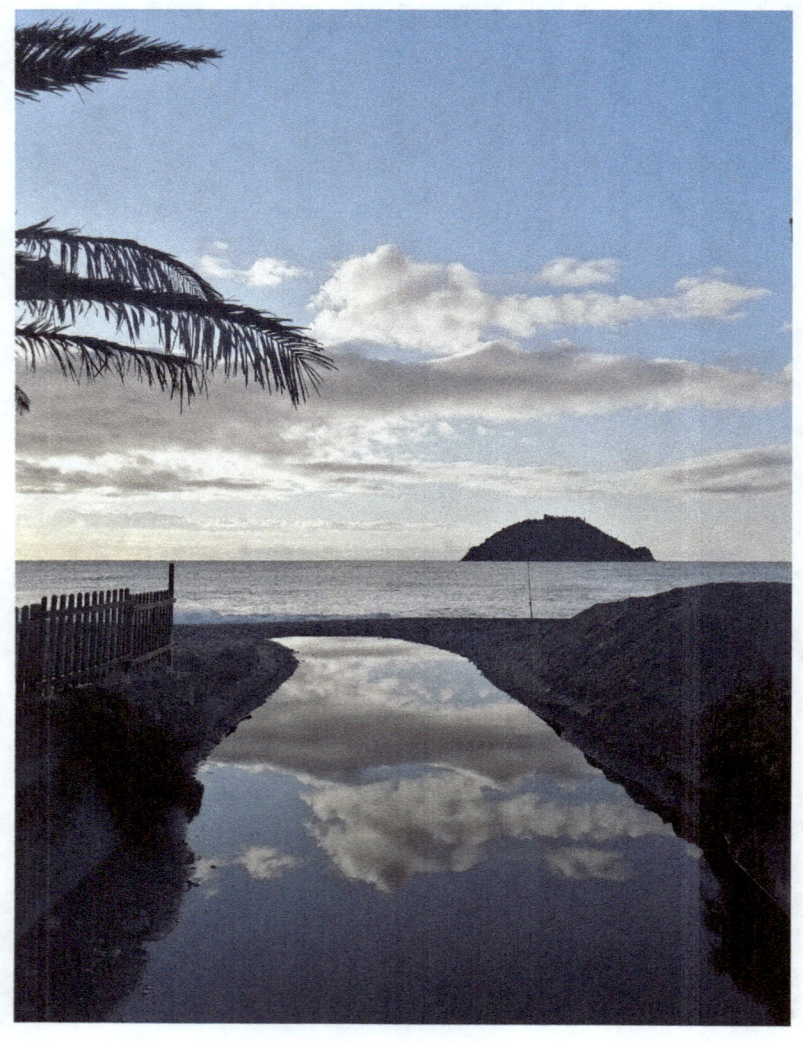

Our eyes try to be swans in the mirror.

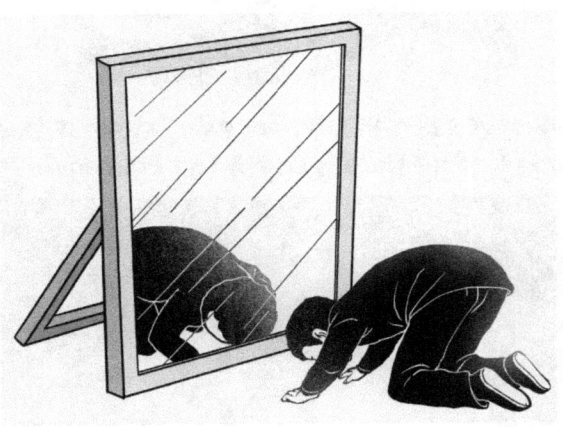

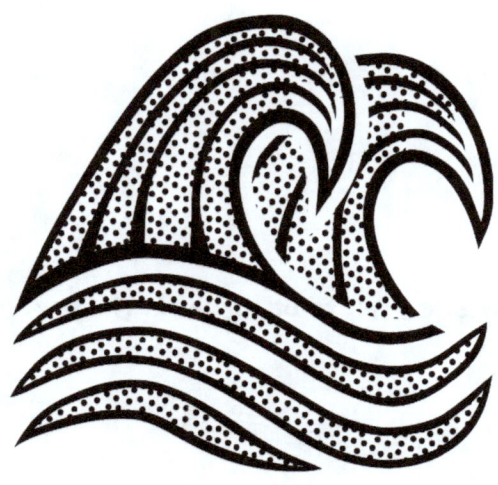

Be like the waves of the sea, breaking against the rocks, but finding the strength to begin again.

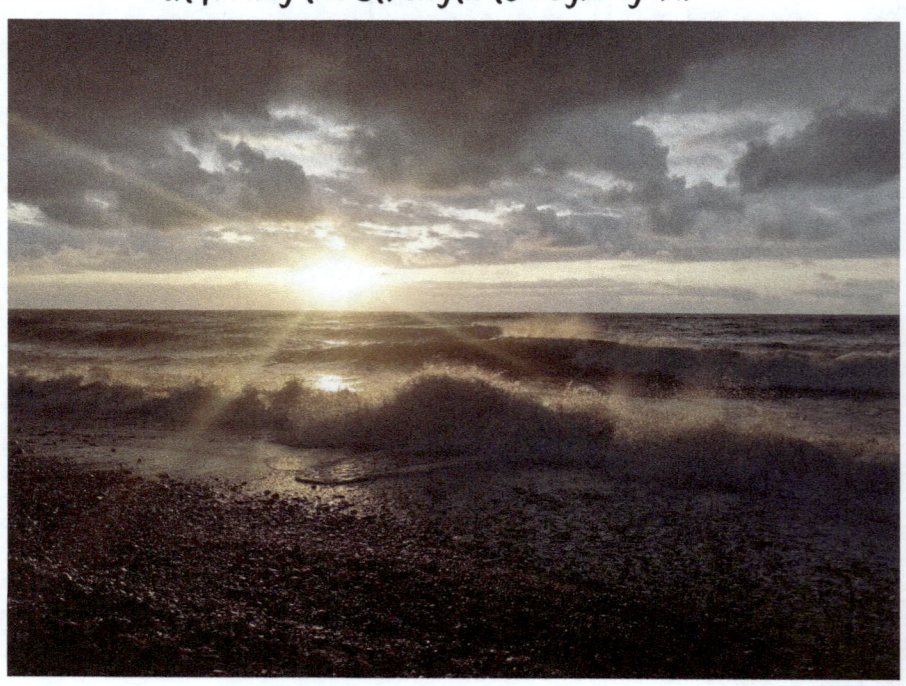

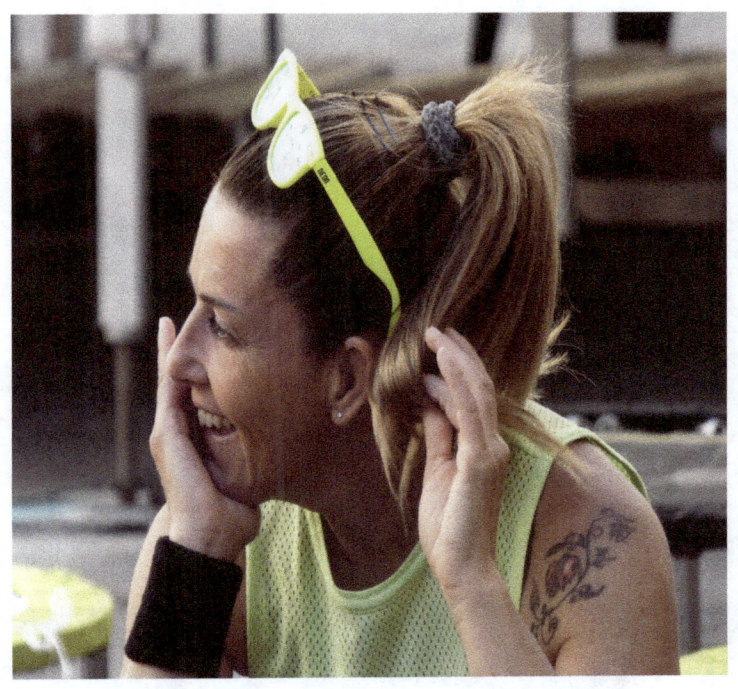

You are not born a woman: You become one.

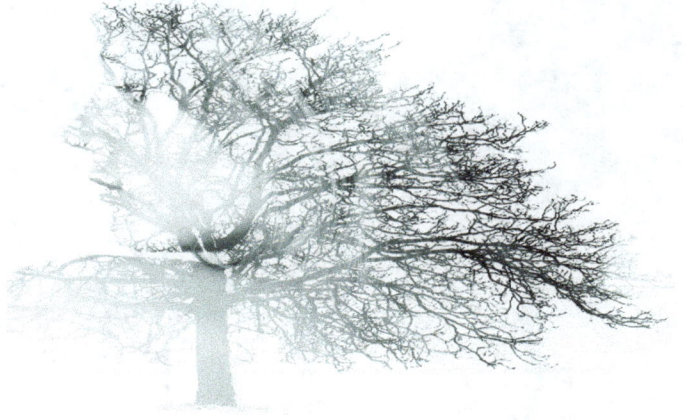

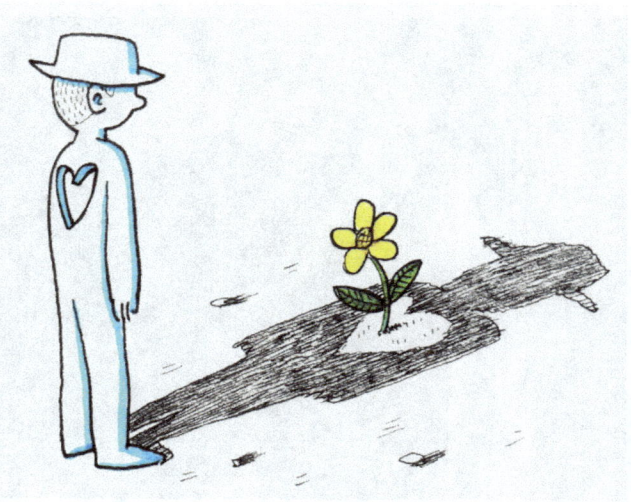

One can live in an idea's shadow without understanding.

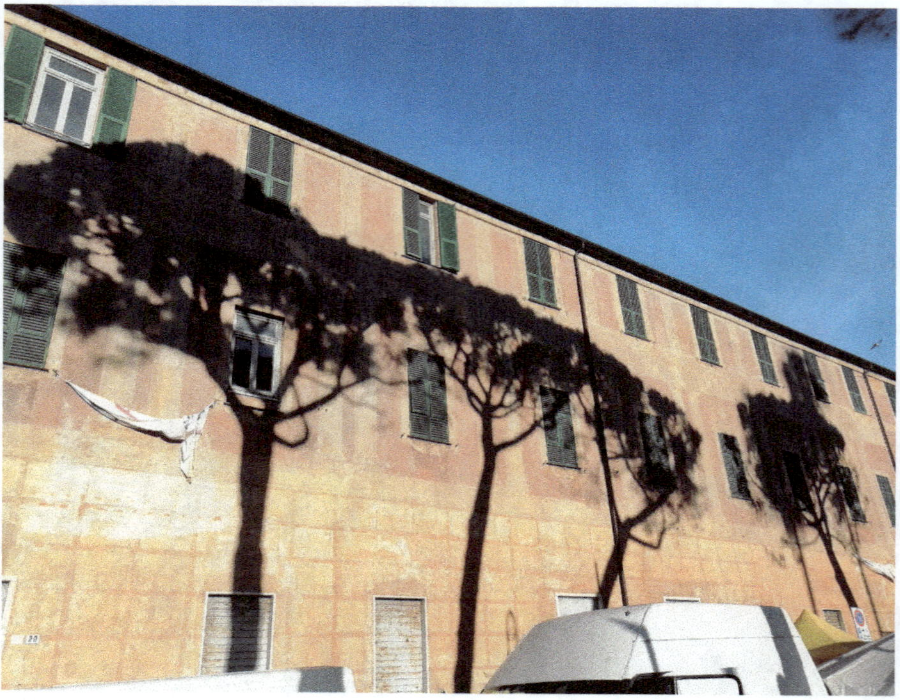

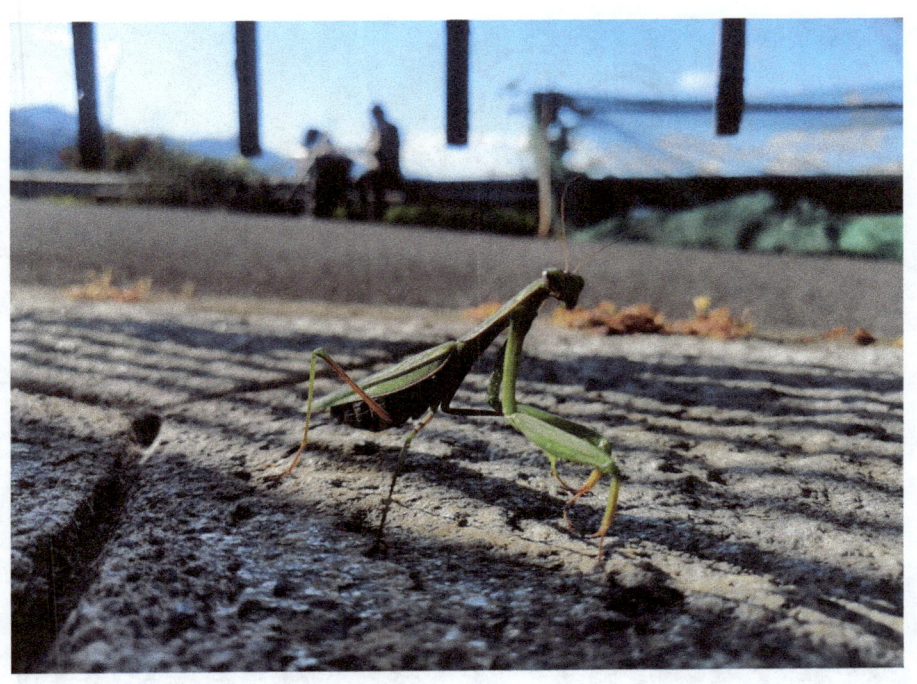

No animal gets used to everything the way humans do.
Except maybe insects.

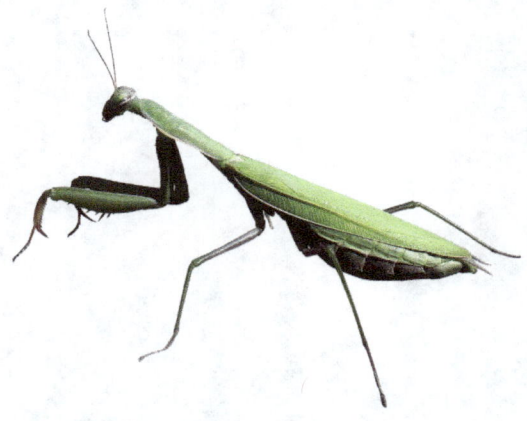

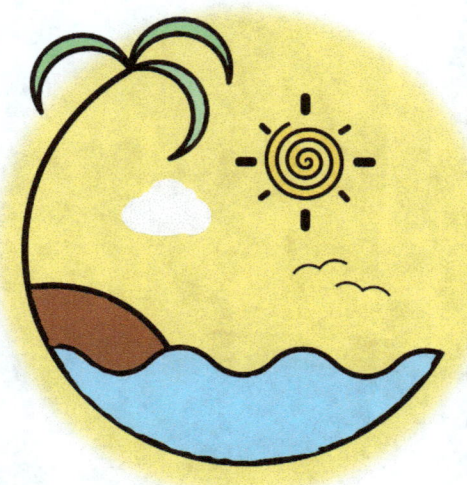

The sun is a friend to be celebrated in spring, avoided in summer, worshipped in autumn and regretted in winter.

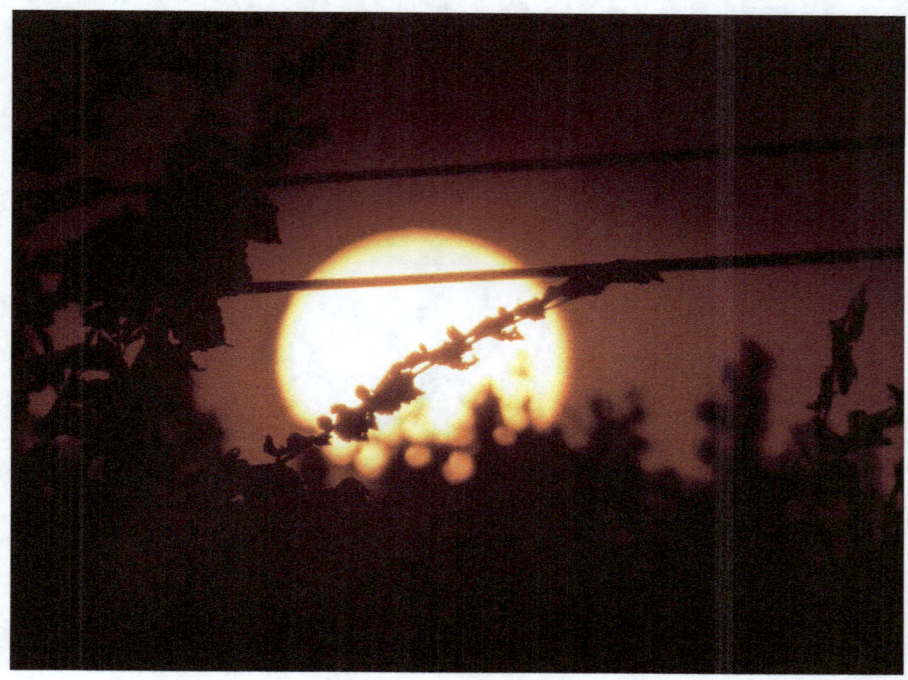

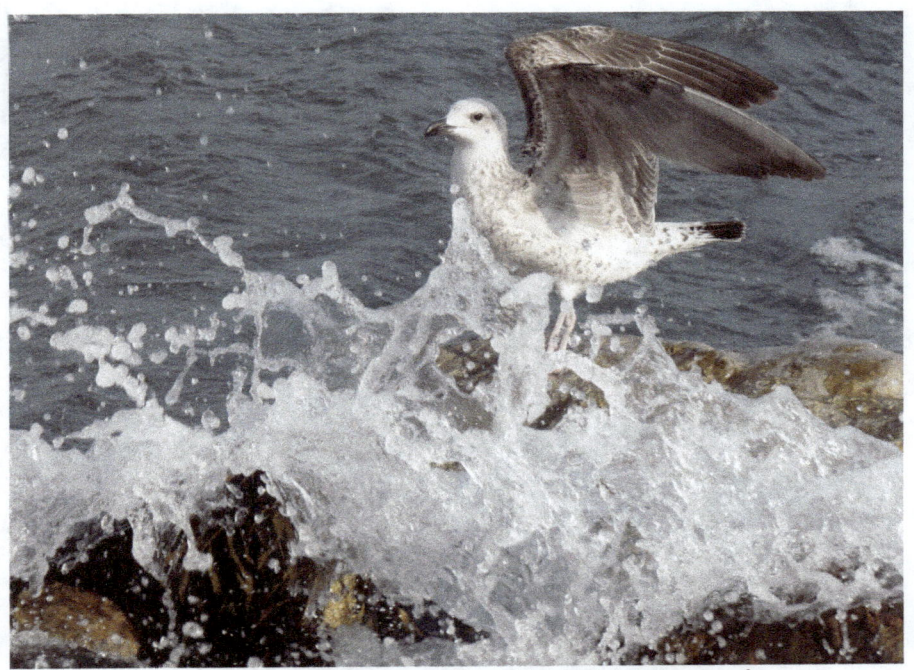

As I watched the seagulls, I thought to myself, this is the way to go; to find the absolute rhythm and to follow it with absolute confidence.

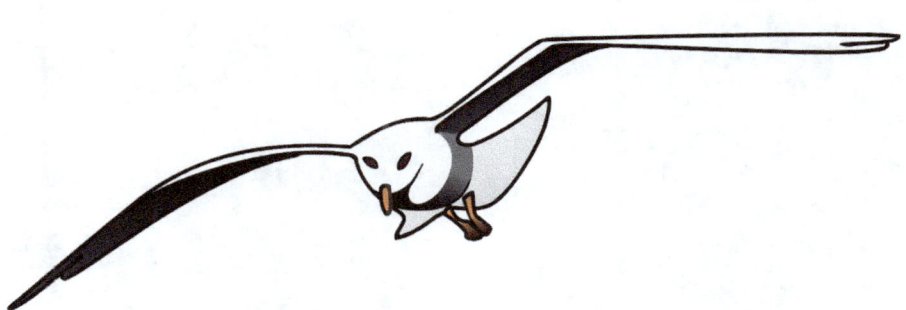

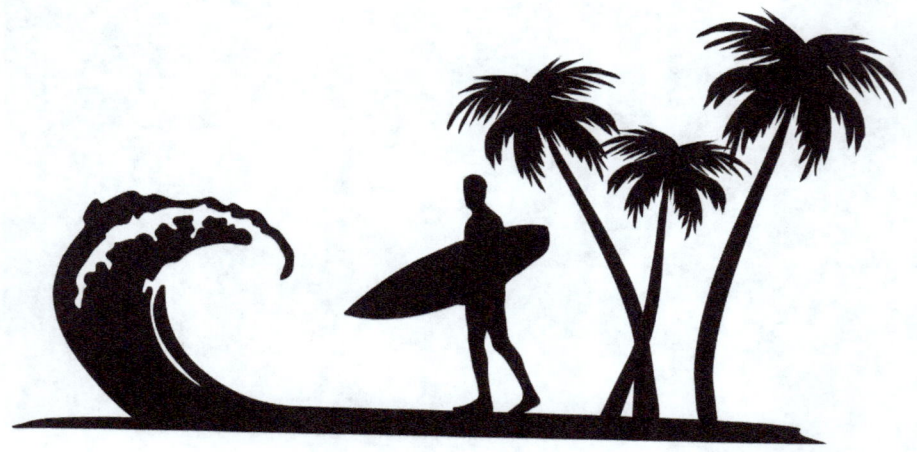

The shore is safer, but I have fun fighting the waves.

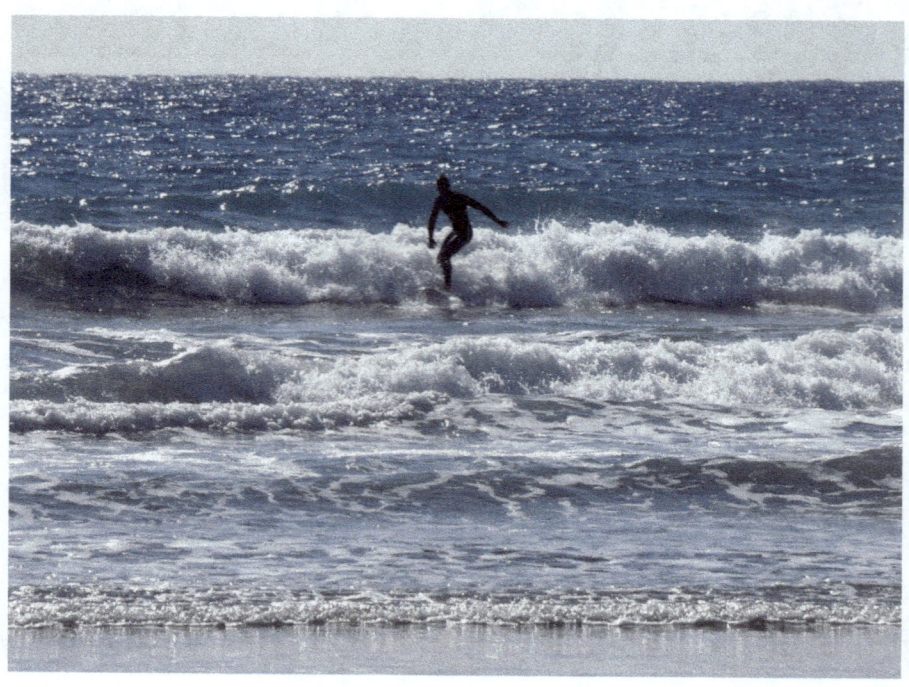

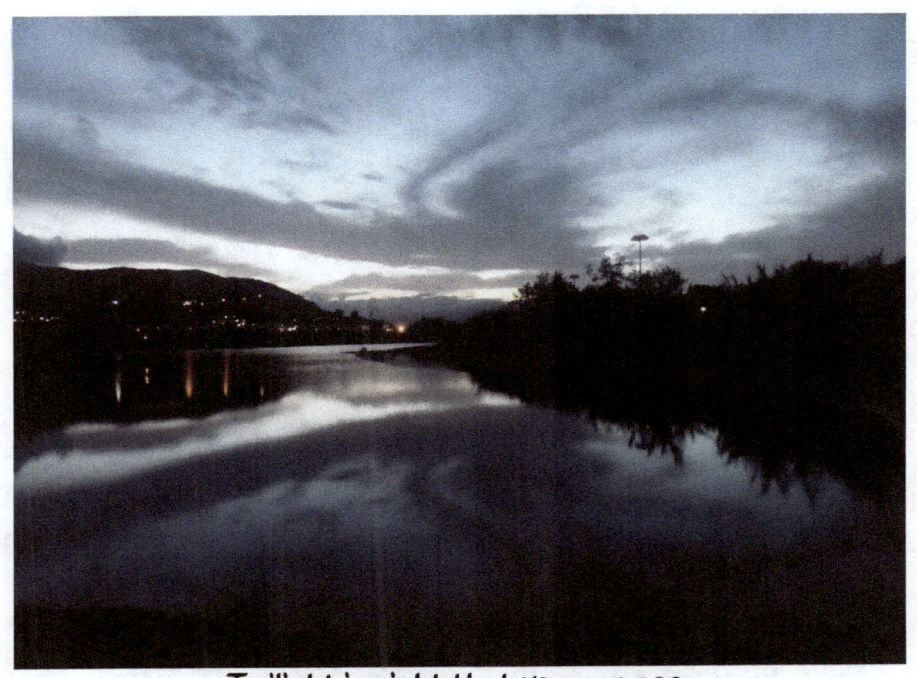

Twilight is night that you can see.

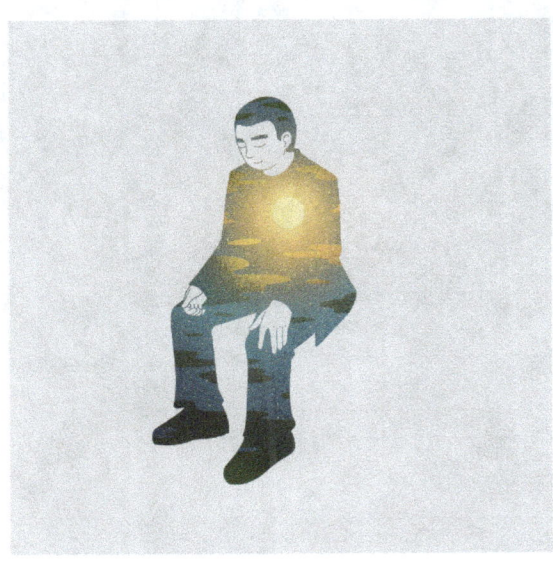

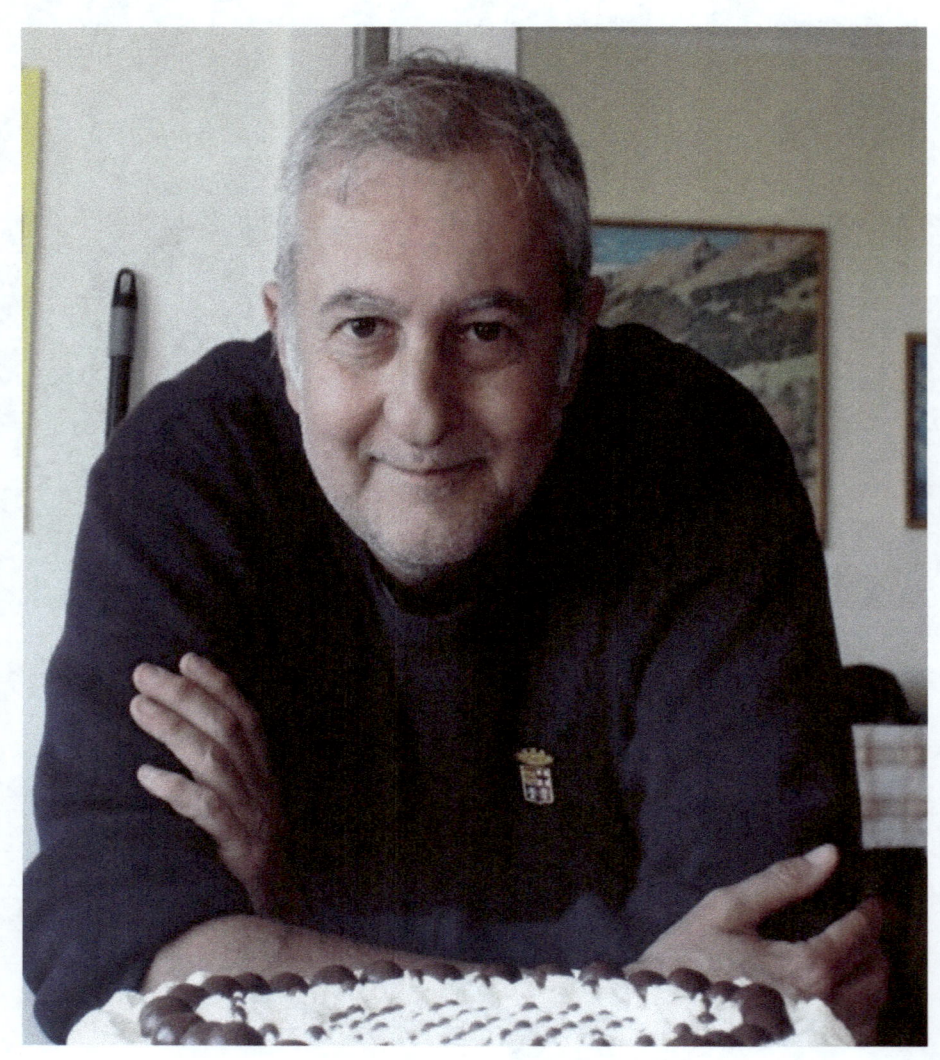

The author

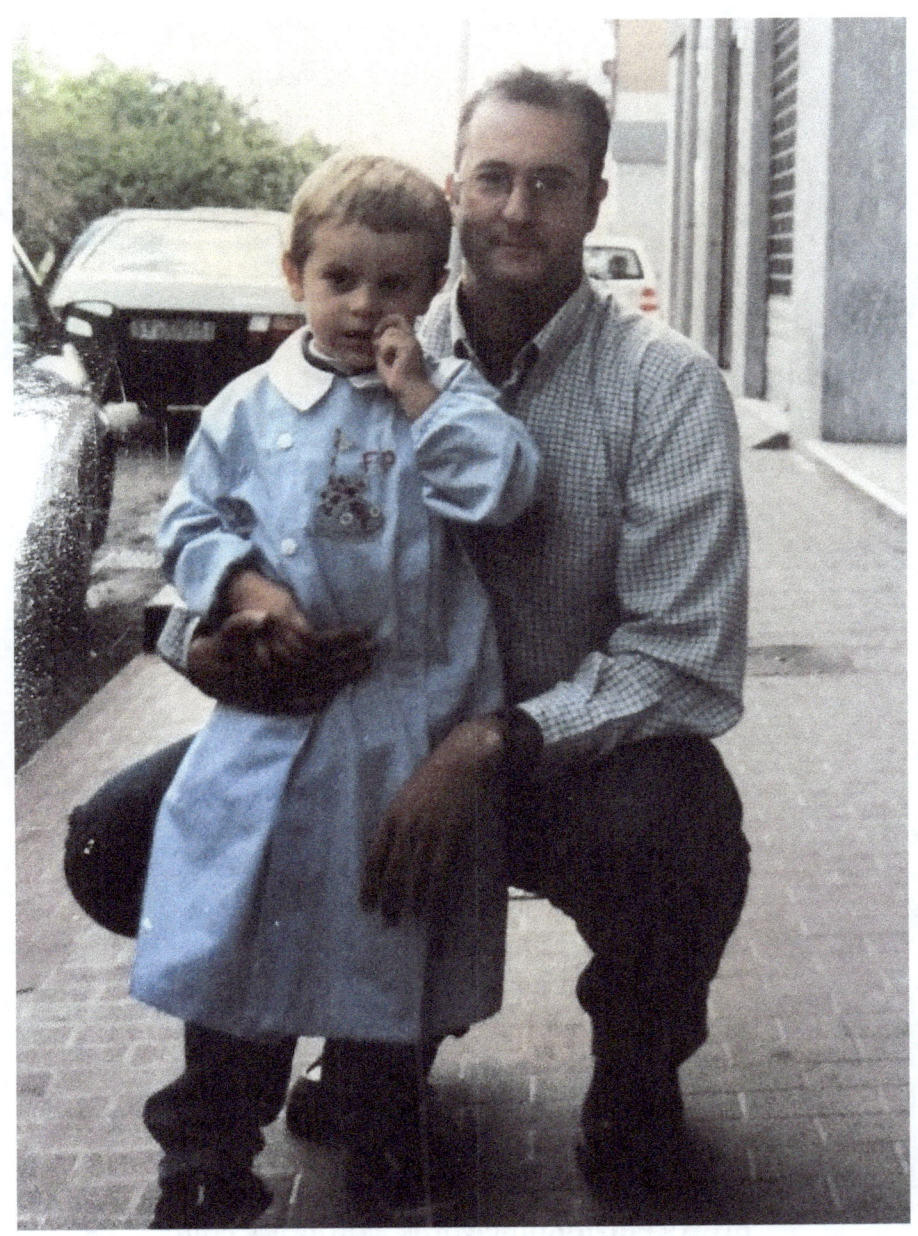

The translator

Literary property of the Author
© 2022, (H)is-land, Roberto RUARO.
Translated by Francesco PANNUTO.
Press. Paprint and Amazon.
You can order manual books,
non-fiction, fiction, poetry,
for children, from the Hogwords Publishing House
by sending an email to edizionihogwords@gmail.com,
by calling 3383229758.
You can find us with the catalog on
https://edizionihogwords.wordpress.com
on Facebook (www.facebook.com/edizionihogwords)
and on https://www.amazon.it/s?k=pier+giorgio+tomatis

www.ingramcontent.com/pod-product-compliance
Lightning Source LLC
Chambersburg PA
CBHW070211230526
45471CB00002B/917